'Pamela Brown-Peterside has written a very thoughtful account which will be full of interest to readers on a number of levels. It touches on matters of theology, Christian growth and community, of race, justice and poverty, and of the making (within the context of Christian faith) of personal identity. It will be engaging to readers today because these issues are covered in an absorbing real-life story. It looks to be a great contribution to contemporary Christian literature.'
*Rev Tim Keller, Founding Pastor, Redeemer Presbyterian Church, NY;* New York Times *best-selling author*

'A heartwarming testimony of one person's journey from the Bronx in New York to a village in Uganda following a calling to serve people with AIDS. The story is both moving and inspirational and will challenge readers to reflect on their own lives and calling, with clear practical examples from the author's own life journey.'
*Ram Gidoomal CBE, Chairman, Traidcraft Plc*

'Pamela Brown-Peterside's work combines vivid description, personal transparency and thoughtful reflection on God's presence, call and work in the world. The author offers a refreshingly direct and honest account of a faithful woman's journey through loss and growth. Her choices to work in contexts of human need and vulnerability and her unusual personal and academic background provide a compelling backdrop for a narrative style that is fast-paced and engaging. It is a vibrant and sobering story that invites readers to reflect on God's redemptive work and their own call and fidelity.'
*Dr Christine D Pohl, Emeritus Professor of Christian Ethics, Asbury Theological Seminary, Wilmore, Kentucky; author*

'Pamela Brown-Peterside's story serves a a
modern-day missionary. One ,
as a West African with transi 1
what it means to be an Africai ;

multiple identities and the true meaning of community in the face of death.

'Pamela's journey, as an Irish-Nigerian who grew up in Nigeria and travelled from the United States to Uganda, echoes a transatlantic voyage. She went as a medical worker to Bundibugyo in Uganda to help pregnant mothers so that the HIV virus would not be transmitted to their babies. In the midst of this was an Ebola breakout that claimed lives. Surrounded by death, Pamela learns the power of community at its finest and what it means to have peace and joy in difficult circumstances.

'This book is recommended to all Christians who want to take their discipleship very seriously and understand what it really means to die to our selfish ambitions.'
*Rev Israel Olofinjana, Founding Director, Centre for Missionaries from the Majority World; author*

'It was Dostoevsky who said that love in practice is a "harsh and dreadful thing" compared to the love in dreams. In this "harsh and dreadful" memoir that includes heartache, loss, sickness and tragedy as she shares her life with the least of these, Pamela provides us with a picture of love in practice. Woven within are also glimpses of hope, redemption, truth, beauty and a love that will not let us go. That is to say, Pamela shows us Jesus. This book is manna for anyone whose imagination is ready to travel to the places where Jesus lives.'
*Rev Scott Sauls, Senior Minister of Christ Presbyterian Church in Nashville; author*

'Pamela Brown-Peterside's journey from HIV work in the South Bronx to a village in Uganda was much more than a long-term mission trip. Her decision to leave behind home and career to return to Africa, the land of her birth, was transformational for the health of the area where she served and for her as an individual and as a Christian. Now chronicled in *African Pearl*, it became not only an eye-opening look at the global health crisis, but also an emotional memoir that takes her from hope to

despair and back to hope, through joy and grief covered with grace, and into depths of loneliness where she finds a profound understanding of community. The lessons and insights she shares are not only for her, but for all who read her wonderful story.'
*Beth Clark, Thinkspot Communications,* New York Times *best-selling writer*

'In a time when so many people of the world are displaced, when crossing cultures is now a daily occurrence wherever you live, we need stories to help us navigate the challenges and gifts of the diversity around us. Dr Pamela Brown-Peterside does that here. But make no mistake: this isn't a "how to" guide for confronting global issues. Rather, this is a beautiful and compelling journey where Pamela leads by example, humbly, carefully and insightfully. It is a story for anyone who cares about loving their neighbour.'
*Jo Kadlecek, author of* Woman Overboard: How Passion Saved My Life

'Pamela Brown-Peterside's book is timely, insightful and important. The stories of the people Pamela met during the AIDS epidemic in Uganda are inspiring, vivid, and deeply moving. *African Pearl* is a compelling read on how Africans are effecting transformative change on their continent, told by an African. This book is a reminder of why Africans must shape their own narratives.'
*Parminder Vir OBE, former CEO, Tony Elumelu Foundation*

# African Pearl

## AIDS, loss and redemption in the shadow of the Rwenzori Mountains

### Pamela Brown-Peterside

instant
apostle

First published in Great Britain in 2020.

Instant Apostle
The Barn
1 Watford House Lane
Watford
Herts
WD17 1BJ

'The Phone Calls' appeared in *Redeemerites*, Number 3, Fall 2010, as 'Dual Drama'. 'The First Ride' was shortlisted for the *Wasafiri* New Writing Prize in 2012 as 'Formidable Women'. 'The Doctor' and 'The Call' appeared in *Kweli.com* as 'The Call' in March 2013. 'The Re-entry' appeared as 'The Clinic' in *Gains and Loses: 21 Stories from the Complete Creative Writing Course,* Maggie Hamand and BB Howe (eds) (London: Barbican Press, 2019). Edited and adapted for this book.

British Library Cataloguing-in-Publication Data

A catalogue record for this book is available from the British Library.

This book and all other Instant Apostle books are available from Instant Apostle:

Website: www.instantapostle.com

Email: info@instantapostle.com

ISBN 978-1-912726-20-2

Printed in Great Britain.

This is based on a true story. However, the timing of some events has been condensed, and, in order to protect people's privacy, some names have been changed.

The pearl of great price is hidden in the field of our life together.

Ruth Haley Barton[1]

# Contents

# Prologue

'There's a strange disease killing people in Kikyo,' Kisembo tells me, a frown spreading across his face. Whenever I go in to pay my bill at his drug shop – the one with a black and white fence a few houses down from Nyahuka Health Centre – if I settle onto a bench and lean my head against the wall, I know I'll get more than just a receipt. This morning I hadn't intended to stay.

'A strange disease? What could it be?' Crossing my legs, I notice the shop smells like damp cardboard, probably due to the recent rains.

'They don't know. Some are saying cholera. Others think typhoid. It's been going on for some two months. So far no response from the Ministry.'

'Eight weeks and they don't know what it is?' I shake my head.

'Only the Bakonjo are dying. People believe the Babwisi are poisoning us.' His voice is strained.

'Kisembo, you know that isn't true,' I say, trying to assure him.

'I know but the people in the mountains, they're not educated, they believe it.' His expression is distant as if his mind's on other things. 'I want to go there, see what's really happening.'

'Good idea.'

'But some of the roads are blocked. The mud is too much. You can't pass. I have to wait.' Worry lines are etched on his forehead. Because he works nights at the hospital as a psychiatric nurse, I'm tempted to attribute his solemnity to a lack of sleep but I don't think that's the case today.

'I've been to Kikyo,' I tell Kisembo, hoping to sound positive. 'Those hills are steep. When I went, I followed a small path. It was very rough. I thought I could manage, but one of my tyres got stuck in a hole.'

His eyes shoot up, revealing a hint of amusement. 'What did you do?'

'A boy wearing a Christ School T-shirt was passing. He helped me.' I smile.

'What were you doing there?'

'Taking mama kits to the health centre. That's what made the *boda boda* so heavy.'

'You took them on your motorcycle?' He raises his eyebrows in disbelief.

'I know. It was foolish. I had gone before with Joseph so I thought I could find my way but I got lost.' Standing, I roll my shoulders backwards a couple of times to loosen the tension there.

'Kisembo, look, I am on my way to Nyahuka. Was just passing when I saw you were open. Can you prepare my bill? I'll come back later.'

'Yes, please.'

'And let me know if there's any more news about that disease.'

He nods.

Stepping out, I mount my bicycle, tuck my skirt around my legs, and cycle carefully, dodging the puddles drenching the path. The lush green of the Rwenzori mountains and the elephant grass on either side of the bridge up ahead are hints of the magnificence I never tire of seeing here. Yet among this breathtaking terrain, death, or talk of death, seems so prevalent. It's as if the beauty is somehow literally taking away people's breath.

Grinding the pedals through the wet sludge makes me winded. I stop for a moment to rest. Standing there with the bike leaning up against me, I can't help thinking that all this loss of life is not what I signed up for. When I decided to come to this remote area of Uganda, I knew I'd be around AIDS patients and that some of them would die, but it didn't occur to me that I'd encounter different kinds of death. Or so much of it.

When does the risk of doing this kind of work become too high, I wonder.

# Part One

Part One

# 1
# The District

Since the terrorist attacks on 11th September 2001, I've become a jittery flier, aware that a journey that seems predictable can give way to tragedy. At the moment, I'm wedged into the cockpit of a five-person Cessna about to take off from Entebbe, Uganda's international airport. Industrial-size headphones flatten my ears, dampening the roar of the engine.

Half an hour ago, when I was standing on the tarmac inhaling fumes and contemplating my first flight in this tiny aircraft, someone called out my name. Turning, I saw three women approaching, all smiling. A slim brunette in jeans stepped forward.

'You must be Pamela. Hi, I'm Jennifer.' She looked more like a carefree postgraduate student than a mother of four in her early forties and the paediatrician half of the doctor couple I'm going to work with for the next three months. Jennifer wrapped her arms around me, and introduced the others. Karen – built like a mature mango tree – enfolded me enthusiastically. Bethany, a younger twenty-something woman, embraced me too.

'Nice to meet you all,' I stammered.

'How was your flight? You came through London?' Jennifer asked.

I nodded. 'Fine. Landed this morning. Then, this afternoon, a man who works at the airport brought me out to the plane.'

'We all just flew in from Nairobi, from a women's conference, which was great,' Jennifer told me. 'Three days without our kids. Really missed them, though.'

'I missed mine too,' chimed in Karen. 'Michael and I have three.'

'Scott and Michael will have had their hands full,' Jennifer grinned. I tried to look sympathetic but couldn't relate. I don't have children.

We're on our way to Bundibugyo, a district on the western border of Uganda, near the Democratic Republic of the Congo, where these women live. The plane taxies down the runway gathering speed, and my heart begins thumping. As we lift off, the ground below us disappearing, my stomach lurches. I throw up a frantic, silent prayer, try to slow down my breathing and will myself to focus on the view. Staring straight ahead, a panorama spanning more than 180 degrees unfolds before us. The city behind us now, I see fertile fields bordering a series of small lakes which shimmer like liquid mirrors. Alongside them, brown terrain resembling a dried-up riverbed becomes visible in the distance. As the plane climbs higher, my tummy settles down. When we level out, our pilot begins talking to me through the mikes attached to our enormous head gear.

'Great day for flying.'

'Yes, the view from up here is unbelievable,' I say. I look over at his red hair and freckles and watch his hands guiding the controls.

'Visibility can change quickly, though,' he tells me. 'The weather too. In about twenty minutes, we'll hit some rain clouds, but it won't last long.'

Right now, this Monday afternoon is radiant with sun and a smattering of fluffy clouds. When we glide through these, the plane hops and dips, and my body protests again, but I discover that seeing the clouds before we fly through them helps to reduce my apprehension.

'How long will it take to get to Bundibugyo?'

'Never been there before, but given the choppy weather ahead, a little over an hour. What do you do there?' He's never flown to Bundibugyo before? My insides do a flip.

'I've never been there either,' I say, slowly. 'I'll be working with an HIV prevention programme. My background's in public health. Will be looking for pregnant women who tested positive then disappeared. They never came back to have their babies.'

'Why look for them?'

'To see how they're doing, and their babies too. When the women found out they had HIV, midwives gave them a pill to take during labour and a dose of syrup for the baby. If mother and baby both got the drugs, most babies should be fine.'

'Didn't know that was even possible.'

'Amazing, isn't it? Most babies born to positive mums don't get HIV. Only about a third do. These drugs cut that down even further.'

'Seems like incredible work.' He glances at me. My lips quiver. It's too early for him to sound impressed. I've not done much yet. Except several months ago, shortly after my fortieth birthday, I left a prestigious public health job in New York City and have now flown half way around the world to the other side of the continent I grew up in to volunteer with a group of Americans I've never met before.

Does that count?

Though this is my first time in Uganda, Africa's no stranger to me. I was born and raised in Jos, a modest city in Nigeria, but my upbringing was hardly typical. Papa was Nigerian, Mum from Northern Ireland, and my four siblings and I were educated at an American missionary school. We learned early on how to navigate multiple cultures on a daily basis and were part of an emerging middle class.

Having lived in Jos until I left home for the US, I've spent little time in rural Africa. More than twenty years ago now, I, like my father, went to university in the States but, unlike him, I eventually settled there. I've returned to Nigeria for regular visits but have not been back to Africa to live.

Suddenly, as the pilot warned, we collide with some turbulence and bounce through the thick grey of a massive cloud. My insides tumble again and the muscles in my upper back tense up, but before my uneasiness settles into fear, the Cessna powers through to the other side, and our vista returns. A quiet breath finds its way out of my lungs.

Conversation ceases but the engine drones on, harsh, dominating, the smell like an overworking generator. After we've been in the air for forty-five minutes, the terrain becomes hillier. Up ahead, the hills give way to mountains.

'The Rwenzoris,' the pilot points out.

'Wow. When I think of snow in Africa, I imagine Kilimanjaro, but I've heard the Rwenzoris not only have Africa's third highest mountain, they have snow on them too.'

As we get closer, the mountains unfold majestically before us, revealing rows and rows of foliage in an array of greens and purples. Soaring over them, however, I see no snow, not even a hint. Disappointed, I wonder what other surprises lie hidden on their slopes.

Leaving the mountains behind and flying low through a valley, we begin descending. Tingling with anticipation, I peer intently at the ground below and am rewarded with my first glimpse of the airstrip, a half-kilometre patch of mowed grass. As we approach and touch down, it extends beneath us like a royal welcome carpet, flanked on either side by thick vegetation. However, there's no terminal, no control tower, and no wind gauge, which couldn't be more of a contrast to the endless concrete of New York City's JFK airport. We taxi to the end of the airstrip adjacent to a dirt road, and there, pressed against waist-high grass are about fifty Ugandans. Most are men and children. The women, I later learn, are working in their gardens. A few white faces are visible, also men and kids. The plane comes to a bumpy stop in front of the crowd.

Releasing his seatbelt, the pilot opens his door. While the others start to file out on his side, he comes around to open mine. A blast of hot air engulfs the cockpit, moistening my armpits. It's early November but I'm glad to be wearing a sleeveless white cotton top and an ankle-length skirt over bare legs. I unstrap myself and stumble down the steps. Trying to appear nonchalant, I push my glasses up on my nose and run my hands through my dark curls. Not sure what to do, I watch the others. My eyes catch Jennifer hugging a tall, lean man. He's dressed in jeans and his hair is a shock of white. Moments later, he approaches, saving me from the awkwardness. He extends his right hand.

'Welcome to Bundibugyo. I'm Scott. Glad you're here, Pamela.' His handshake is solid.

'Thanks. Me too.'

We retrieve the luggage, pile into three four-wheel-drive vehicles, and pull away from the airstrip. Palm trees, grass tall enough to hide elephants, and acacia bushes line the dirt road. The mountains, to our left, are on the same side that we're driving on. They seem close because they are, as if forming a barrier for this faraway place. Winston Churchill called Uganda the 'Pearl of Africa' and I'm beginning to see why. Its beauty has a raw, arresting quality, like an attractive woman who doesn't know the power of her captivating good looks. She's already seducing me, helping me to forget – at least for now – about the insidious virus lurking in this community that I've come to help tackle.

Beyond the physical beauty, my eyes are drawn to the people. Most women are wrapped in bright, colourful pieces of material, rather than fitted dresses, many with babies on their backs. Others are walking with infants; some are balancing firewood or a basket on their heads. Men stroll along, wearing slacks and Western-style tops. I notice an Arsenal and then a Manchester United shirt, presumably sent abroad from charity shops in England. I see school-age children in blue uniforms, many laughing together, a few carrying notebooks. Girls wear their hair closely cropped; they are distinguishable only by their skirts. Smaller children who aren't wearing uniforms are in tattered clothes. Some have nothing on except a pair of worn underpants or shorts. Few are wearing shoes or sandals. Many smile or wave as we pass them. As I observe these Ugandans, excitement bubbles inside me. I'm definitely back in Africa again.

After ten minutes of non-stop jostling over rough terrain and around several blind curves – the road far worse than any I've travelled on before – we pull into a driveway that wraps around a mango tree. The Nissan Patrol stops in front of a large house with unpainted cinder-block walls and cheerful blue shutters on either side of the windows. Blue screen-covered doors are at both ends of the building. I hop out after Bethany.

'Follow me,' she says. 'I'll let you in on my side.' We head to the far door, where she unlocks a hefty padlock, and step into a room empty except for a long bench against a wall. Bethany kicks off her slippers. 'This is the greeting room where we see visitors. You can leave your shoes here.' I take off my sandals, sticky with sweat. Cool cement floors soothe my soles. Past a curtain, Bethany leads me into an open sitting-dining room next to an exposed kitchen. Beyond the dining table is a door that's ajar.

'You'll stay with Pat, through here. She's driving back from Kampala tomorrow since there wasn't space on the plane.' We pass through the doorway into another living-dining-kitchen area identical to Bethany's. 'Here's where you'll be.' She motions to the back corner on the right.

The room has two large windows with wooden shutters, wire screens and horizontal bars, but no glass. The furniture is basic but looks comfortable: a simple desk, a dozen hangers strung across a pole hanging from the ceiling, and a narrow bed encased in a white mosquito net. I lift the net and ease myself onto the bed.

'I'll let you unpack. Shout if you need anything,' Bethany calls out before disappearing.

Sinking onto the mattress, I exhale, grateful to have come this far. I close my eyes, eager to rest. I'd like to linger, even lie down for a short nap, but there isn't time. Scott and Jennifer have invited me to dinner. So, after using the toilet, which I discover is a latrine outside at the back, and hanging up my few clothes, I splash cold water on my face, get directions from Bethany, and head back out – for my first supper with my new bosses.

# 2
# The End of the Road

Scott and Jennifer's house glows like a small city perched on a hill. Though the sun is beginning to disappear, those are the only lights I see. I'm reminded that solar batteries power the missionary homes, something I heard before I got here. Keeping the brightness in view, I follow a worn path through a loose collection of unpainted buildings, and cross the road. A hedge fencing the yard leads to a small roundabout. Beside it is a trellis bursting with magenta bougainvillea flowers and chirping crickets, and beyond that a bungalow. I approach a screen door where the hint of something baking drifts out.

'Come on in,' says Jennifer, looking through the mesh wire as I'm about to knock. She's standing in front of an old-fashioned gas stove. Her brown wavy hair is damp and has formed wet stains on the shoulders of her T-shirt.

'Thanks,' I say, stepping inside. 'Is that bread baking? I love that smell.'

'Every day. We have it with dinner and then use the leftovers for the kids' lunches. We eat a lot in this family.' She smiles at me. 'Have a seat.'

I move past a counter which is in front of two long benches with backrests. They flank a dining table that's already set. Beyond it is a small living room, with a rug covering the cement floor, and four easy chairs. Their simplicity suggests they were made in Uganda. Two school-age boys, both with straight, wet hair, each engrossed in a book, are seated there in front of several overstuffed bookcases.

'Jack, Caleb, this is Miss Pamela. She'll be helping with the Kwejuna Project.'

They glance at me, mumble a quick hello, and resume reading.

'Jack's six and Caleb is nine. You'll meet Luke and Julia when we sit down to eat.'

'Jennifer, how can I help?'

'We're almost ready. Have a seat,' she says again.

I plop onto a chair next to the boys, pretending to be relaxed though I'm shy and withdrawn and hardly know this family. Except for a phone call with Scott to set up this trip, and a few emails from Jennifer, we've had no other contact. Still, I know a few basic facts about them. Together, they co-lead a team of singles and families affiliated with World Harvest, a Christian organisation located in suburban Philadelphia. Working among the very poor, team members live here for stretches of time, from a few months, like me, to others who've been here more than ten years. Several minutes after I sit, Scott enters carrying a bottle of red wine.

'Would you like some?'

'Sure,' I say, raising my eyebrows. 'Do they sell that here?'

'No, not yet.' He fills three glasses. 'Beer and soft drinks, but not wine. This comes from Kampala. Every six to eight weeks, we leave the district to stock up on foods we can't get here. Rice, pasta, cheese, frozen chicken, things like that.'

Jennifer explains, 'We joke that when chicken cutlets make their way over the mountains, it'll be time for us to leave. That won't happen until the government brings electricity and paves the road. Every few years, there's talk of that, but either the contracts aren't awarded or the money disappears. You know how that goes.' She glances at me.

They seat me at the head of the table. Scott sits at the other end. The two kids I haven't met come in and sit across from each other. Jennifer, Jack, and Caleb join us.

'Luke, Julia, this is Miss Pamela,' Jennifer tells them.

'Hi, Miss Pamela,' says Julia, who has freckles and is missing a tooth in the top row of her mouth.

'Hello,' mutters Luke, looking away. I wonder if he's shy or perhaps just distracted.

I notice more wet hair and take in a whiff of soap. Everyone has bathed, except me. Dust and heat have stained my top. My lined skirt clings to my calves. I realise, too late for tonight, that being clean is a pre-dinner ritual here.

The meal that evening reminds me of a favourite Manhattan restaurant. Jennifer serves a chicken and bow-tie pasta dish with green peppers, string beans, carrots and basil grown in their garden. Dessert is a home-made brownie. Listening to the kids bantering with one another, I struggle to follow along but do my best to make eye contact.

'What will you be doing again?' Caleb asks at one point, as if suddenly remembering I'm there.

'Helping with the Kwejuna Project.'

'She'll be going out on *boda bodas* looking for women in Kwejuna,' Scott explains.

'Do you know how to ride a motorcycle?' asks Julia, her eyes round with curiosity.

'No,' I say, laughing. 'I'll need to hire one. I'll always be on the back.'

When the meal is over, the children scatter. Jennifer calls after them, reminding them to tidy their rooms. The three of us clear the table. As we do, I hear myself say, 'I didn't expect to eat so well here. Thank you. That was delicious.'

'We try to make your first meal special,' says Jennifer. 'When we came, things were very different. This house wasn't built. Luke was only seven months. We ate sitting on folding chairs around a small card table. We want to make sure new people have a different experience.' Putting water on to boil, she continues, 'Eating well is tricky but it's a priority. Having good food is one way for us to cope with how hard life can be here – the poverty, endless needs, many deaths.'

'Deaths from AIDS?'

'Lots of kids die from malaria. Sickle cell. Malnutrition too. They're the biggest killers. A few die of AIDS, but something else usually kills them long before that.'

Once the water boils, Scott begins to wash the dishes. Jennifer sets up to rinse. Watching them together side by side, I'm struck by how foreign this was in my childhood home. Like many Nigerian fathers, Papa never washed the plates and seldom even ventured into the kitchen except to make Mum tea every morning, before anyone else was awake.

'How long have you been in Bundibugyo?' I ask.

'We came here in the fall of 1993,' Jennifer tells me. 'Nyahuka was much smaller then.'

'Eleven years ago? Wow. What's Nyahuka?'

Scott chimes in, 'It's the trading centre past the mission, less than a kilometre from here. In the early years, Nyahuka really felt like we were living at the end of the road.'

The irony of being at the end of the road for where I feel in my own life isn't lost on me: burned out from the AIDS job I left in the Bronx and not sure what to do next after this short stint is over. But I don't dare share these thoughts with them. It's too early for that.

Scott continues, 'There was nothing much beyond Nyahuka except the Congo border six kilometres away. It was really hard in the beginning.' He glances uneasily at Jennifer. She doesn't notice. 'We didn't speak the language and medically things were so different from how we'd been trained. We started working at the hospital, in Bundibugyo Town.'

Jennifer picks up the story. 'But once I had the other kids, going all the way there – a thirty-minute drive and back again every day over that road – it got to be too much. We had four of them in five years, something I tell mothers here *not* to do.' She laughs. 'I'm the reason you should use birth control.' Not sure if I should chuckle too, I offer a weak smile.

Scott goes on to explain about their work. 'Switching to the health centre at Nyahuka made more sense. It has a lot less staff and a much smaller budget but sees almost as many patients. We felt we could have more of an impact there.'

'How did you end up coming to Bundibugyo?' I ask. 'It's beautiful but seems so remote.'

Jennifer empties the dirty rinse water and refills her basin. 'The mission was interested in starting churches here because there were none, but those who came in the mid-eighties to do that discovered Bundibugyo was so poor.'

Scott continues, 'So the mission realised we couldn't just focus on saving people's souls. We had to address their practical needs too. Jennifer and I came to develop a community health programme. Around the same time the mission built a secondary school, Christ School, because this district had the worst school results in the whole of Uganda. We have a water programme too.' He goes on, 'We have a lot of different things going on, but our main goal is to love Ugandans well.'

I lean back against the counter, intrigued about what it means to 'love Ugandans well'. Until now, I've thought of missionaries as one-dimensional, boring even. This couple hardly seem like that. Wondering how Jennifer juggles parenting and doctoring, I ask about her typical day.

'I do rounds in the morning. I'll take you with me tomorrow. After lunch, I catch up on email, help the kids with their homework. Sometimes patients stop by. Then I make dinner.'

I remain quiet. I've barely had the strength to get myself to and from a desk job in the Bronx. Where does she get the energy to care for sick children, parent four kids, and cook delicious meals?

With the washing finished, Scott moves over to help with drying. 'My day's a little different. I'm a family practice doc. Don't do rounds any more but still go to Nyahuka a couple days a week to do sonograms for our HIV-positive mothers. The Kwejuna Project keeps me busy,' he says flashing a smile at me. 'Besides that, all kinds of things come up every day.'

'When you come here, you end up doing far more than what you think you'll be doing,' adds Jennifer. I doubt I'll be here long enough for that to be true for me. 'It's a rich life but involves sacrifice. Raising our kids so far away from our families is one of them. They miss out on so much not being in the States. It's especially tough as our parents get older.' She turns away, shielding her eyes, before lifting a serving dish to dry.

Swallowing hard, I think about the many sacrifices my mum made forty-five years ago: marrying Papa in London when he was a poor student, coping with her parents' disapproval, and going to live in Nigeria in the early sixties, which meant raising us thousands of miles from her Northern Irish relatives before international phone calls or long-haul flights were affordable.

When the dishes are all put away, Jennifer leads us to a large room on the other side of their kitchen. It's an octagonal-shaped space with orange parquet-style tiles, filled with chairs and couches. A lone overhead bulb sits above an electric piano, which must be possible because of their solar power. The rest of the lights in here come from candles attached to each wall in gecko-shaped candlestick holders. Shadows from the flames flicker like traditional dancers.

Jennifer pulls up a wicker chair for me. 'Enough about us. We want to hear about you. What's your story?'

Not sure how much to tell them, I hesitate and begin talking.

# 3
# The Bronx

The decision to leave my job in the Bronx came abruptly, though it had been building. Six months before I found myself in Uganda, a blaring siren interrupted me on a spring afternoon while I was reviewing a report. Looking out of my large window facing Third Avenue, clogged with rush-hour traffic, I saw an ambulance crawling towards the three-way intersection called the Hub at 149th Street. Watching it inch along through the congestion, I realised I felt as trapped as that vehicle. Weariness had settled into my thirty-nine-year-old bones.

When I first started here almost a decade ago, this job had stretched me in good ways. I was hired as the director of a new grant-funded investigative clinic in the South Bronx, the poorest congressional district in the US. The goal was to involve women from the area as part of an effort to find a preventive vaccine for HIV. Before introducing any experimental products, we began by conducting surveys and providing HIV counselling and testing at six-month intervals, following the same group of women for eighteen months.

Those we recruited had limited resources and most were African-American or Latina, which reflected our location. We'd simply followed the virus. This zip code, 10456, located with others nearby, was one of three areas in New York City with the highest rates of HIV infection for women in the mid-1990s.

Many of the women we worked with were recovering crack addicts. When they failed to show up, Yvonne, our outreach worker, would go out in a taxi to search for them. Venturing into housing projects and along dark hallways, this youthful-looking Puerto Rican grandmother slipped missed appointment letters under doors. Sometimes, an apartment would be burned down, or bolted shut, indicating eviction. Then, Yvonne became a detective, trying to track down where our clients had gone.

To follow women on the fringes of drug addiction for months at a time, we developed informal case management strategies and provided referrals for housing, domestic violence and drug treatment. Still, the women's needs were like the drip-drip-drip of a defective tap and the work was draining. However, despite a couple of thefts in the office, some relapses back to crack, and several women becoming HIV infected, we persevered. The setting was far from glamorous and the challenges were many, but the four employees I line managed were committed and hard-working. We all felt strongly that despite the extra effort it required, women in this community deserved to participate in this cutting-edge research because we hoped they and others like them would eventually benefit from a licensed vaccine.

Through a lot of determination, hard work and old-fashioned tender loving care, we managed to remain in touch with the initial group of women for those first eighteen months. We received funding for more studies, but our efforts took a toll. In quick succession, three employees decided they had had enough. One by one they left. I replaced them and we soldiered on. Yvonne remained, providing an important point of continuity for the women. I promoted her. Our site gained respect. Colleagues in our research network began to seek us out as the 'experts' who knew what it took to work with high-risk women. We published a few papers and I presented our work at conferences. We relocated to this larger space. Those were heady days.

Over time, though, due to tackling the numerous decisions that are inherent in overseeing a small team with limited resources and an expanding workload, the enthusiasm I started with began to wane. Staff turnover continued to be high, and sometimes I instigated it. After each departure, it took longer for us to rebuild as a team. Recently, I'd found myself questioning the commitment of another employee. Her work was beginning to suffer and I was starting to doubt myself. Could her absenteeism become grounds for another dismissal, or was this about me? Was I losing compassion for those I worked with?

Looking around my office that day, listening to the screech of that siren, I wondered how long I could keep going. Besides managing the site, pressure was growing from my boss for me to join her in bringing in funds to support our work. I had written several small applications for foundation grants that were successful, but my first major proposal was turned down and I couldn't find the motivation to revise it. The malaise I was feeling was linked to profound disappointment, yes, and even a degree of shame that I'd been unsuccessful in securing the prestigious grant, but it went deeper than that. My lack of motivation had transformed itself into apathy.

When I failed for the third time to focus on the words I was trying to read and the page remained a blur, suddenly it clicked.

I had had enough.

I couldn't face resubmitting the grant application because I'd lost interest in trying to reimagine how to reach at-risk women. Nor could I muster up the energy it would take to dismiss another employee. I sighed and felt a hint of relief. Shoving the report into a folder, I turned off my laptop, slid it into a drawer and locked my desk. Then I grabbed my coat and headed out into the noise and the traffic, convinced, this time, I had to be the one to leave.

Six weeks later, in the middle of June, and with great trepidation, I invited my boss to lunch. Her office, at the New York Blood Center's headquarters on the Upper East Side of

Manhattan, the wealthiest neighbourhood in the city at the time, was only a twenty-minute subway ride away from the deprivation of the South Bronx. However, the economic gulf couldn't have been greater. As we took our seats in a trendy bistro with the sun streaming in through the windows, my heart was beating so loudly I feared it would give me away.

'I have something to tell you,' I began, after we'd ordered, fidgeting with the linen napkin folded at our place mats. She met my eyes but said nothing.

'I've decided to leave,' I blurted out. Her expression didn't change but her face went grey, the same way it did the only time I'd seen her angry. Looking away, I felt tears fill my eyes. Grief I didn't realise was there began to overwhelm me. The fear of letting go of a stable job with predictable relationships to enter a future that was unknown and frightening seized me. But it was out now. There was no turning back. I began to weep, and try as I might, I couldn't contain the sadness. I brushed tears away before they could fall and wiped my nose with the back of my hand.

'I strongly believe in including poor women of colour in HIV vaccine trials and behavioural studies,' I sniffled. 'And I'm really proud of what we've done together.' I hesitated before continuing. 'But I'm exhausted,' I whispered. Fishing around for a tissue in my bag, I dug one out and blew my nose. 'I can't keep doing this any more, because the truth is, I'm burned out.' Her gaze didn't change, though the colour returned to her face. 'It's been a really hard decision because it's such important work, and it needs to continue.' She nodded. 'I just can't be the one doing it.'

I don't think she saw my decision coming when it did, but she was gracious and understanding, and she got it. She could tell my mind was made up and there was no point in trying to persuade me to change it. Though revealing all of this to her was unsettling, once I dried my eyes and pulled myself together, I was ready to get practical and consider next steps. By the time we finished our meal, we'd begun to strategise about the timing of my exit and when I'd tell the staff.

I resigned a couple of weeks later at the end of the month and gave three months' notice. I wanted to transition out slowly, wrap up a qualitative research project I was leading, and give us all time to prepare for what would come next.

I wasn't worried about the work in the Bronx continuing. I had confidence it would go on, especially when my boss agreed to promote someone on my team who was very capable, but as my end date approached, I became increasingly nervous about my future. Despite the fact that I was the one choosing to leave, I was terrified of letting go of the professional trajectory I'd been scaling up. What had helped to push me out was a very real fear of getting to the end of my working life and regretting that I hadn't had the courage to see what else might be out there, what else God might have in store for me. Still, the fact remained, I was moving on without a clear plan and this propelled me into a quiet state of panic. As the desperation mounted, I began soliciting advice from anyone who would listen, which was quite unlike me.

Have you ever thought about Uganda?

My heart stirred when I read that one-line email. Uganda was far away from New York; better still, it was Africa; and even better, it was somewhere on the continent I'd never been to before. That's how I found myself on a bench in the shade of Central Park on a muggy summer afternoon talking with Katherine. In her early fifties with blonde highlights, Katherine was someone I was just getting to know. We had met a few times through mutual friends at church.

'You should go to Bundibugyo, to work with two doctors there who're doing great work,' she said, her turquoise eyes resting on mine.

'Bundi what?' I asked. Katherine sounded so sure of herself. I envied her confidence and the ease with which this strange name rolled off her tongue. Several years before, Katherine had left a successful career as a CEO in Silicon Valley to start a

Center for Faith and Work at our church. The centre was one of the first of its kind, engaging Christians in the workplace and gathering people in similar fields to wrestle with how to integrate their faith into areas as diverse as financial services, education, healthcare, and the arts.

One Sunday in July – after I'd handed in my notice – we'd found ourselves travelling together on the same subway heading home. Our seat on that 'A' train was as grey and murky as my future seemed to be.

'I'm leaving my public health job at the end of September,' I told Katherine, my heart heavy, my mind a jumble of fragmented thoughts. 'After nine years, I'm weary. It's lonely being in charge and I don't want that responsibility any more.'

'What are you going to do next?' she asked.

'I'm thinking of a sabbatical,' I said, eager for her insight and wisdom. 'Maybe take a few months off before getting into something new. Any ideas about how to use that time?' Though I was trying to sound like I had a game plan, in reality it was a cover-up. I had no idea what to do next. What I yearned for was a complete break. Besides, I knew that leaving one taxing job and moving straight into a new position wouldn't give me the chance to recover, rest or regroup.

'A sabbatical? Interesting.' Her stare seemed kind even if it was penetrating. 'I'll pass along anything that comes across my desk.' I couldn't tell if she was being polite, but at least she wasn't dismissive.

Turns out her offer to help had been a serious one.

'Bundi what?' I repeated, leaning forward.

She laughed. A faraway look spread across her face. 'Bundibugyo. It's beautiful, but I could never live there. You could, since you grew up in Nigeria.' Warmth rushed to my face and not because of the thick summer humidity: I felt a sense of excitement and anticipation. She went on, 'These doctors, a couple, just got a grant to start an AIDS programme for women. They're swamped. You could help them.'

'How do you know?' I asked.

'I get their letters. My brother and his family used to live there. I went to visit a few times.'

'You've been there?' She had my full attention now.

Katherine nodded. 'I didn't want my nieces and nephew to grow up without them knowing who I was.' Her voice intensified. 'You'd love it. You'd love working with Scott and Jennifer, but you'd also be with a team. You'd have community.' As she made her case, I wondered if she could detect how miserable I was. The demands of my job had sucked the joy out of me like a punctured tyre with a slow, imperceptible leak. I sensed this tyre needed replacing, but until I heard about the prospect of a total escape from New York, only then did I allow myself to admit something I knew deep down. The realisation surfaced stubbornly like a body floating on the Dead Sea. My need was far greater than a new tyre: I required a complete service overhaul.

Being far from here would provide me with much-needed perspective. And it would give me a taste of what it would be like to work in an African setting, something I'd wanted to experience ever since I studied public health. My heart rate began to speed up. My head felt weightless. I was beginning to like the sound of this Uganda idea.

Then Katherine said, 'You'll need to raise money.'

'Raise money? What do you mean?' I asked. The light-headedness dissipated.

'You'll need to get people to give financially to this, and you'll need people who give not just money, but who'll pray for you every day while you're there.' As she'd talked, I'd assumed I'd pay for a ticket with my modest savings, volunteer for a few months, and return to New York City with a clear head, ready to transition into a less stressful job.

Katherine continued, 'You'd be joining a team of missionaries. They all raised funds to go there. Even though you'd be going short term, you'd have to do the same.'

Missionaries? It was as if I'd been punched. Forty-five years ago, missionaries had started the American boarding school we attended. I'd never given it much thought before now, but I knew they'd raised money, mostly from churches, to support them in their work. Our family was among a small minority of non-missionaries who went to the school and paid our own way. We received a solid education, but often felt like outsiders because our parents worked in secular jobs and we lived at home. Now, more than two decades later, I remained ambivalent about that experience, and about missionaries.

Still, I couldn't deny the fact that missionaries were the ones who had introduced me to the Christian faith as a child, something I'd made my own first as a teenager and then again in my early thirties after drifting away from Jesus at university. Nor could I ignore that this renewed commitment to believe in a loving, personal God who'd lived and died for me and been resurrected from the dead, had changed my life. But this decision to go to Uganda didn't just mean I'd have to work with missionaries, it also meant having to ask people to give their hard-earned money for me to do this.

These conflicting thoughts hurled towards me once I realised Katherine's idea was tied both to missionaries and to fund-raising. However, by the time this came up, I was so persuaded by the prospect of what I'd have the opportunity to do that I was willing to tolerate the missionary aspect of it. How bad could that be? After all, this programme in rural Uganda, in the heart of the global AIDS epidemic, would offer me a different kind of HIV prevention experience, expanding my public health exposure. It might also help me to rediscover fulfilment in my life's work, something that now felt so out of reach. And, having a specific plan would soften my exit from the Bronx. This was in many ways a wonderful opportunity. So, in those moments, I decided if I had to ask people for money, I could just about manage that. I reckoned I could always rely on my own funds if the money didn't come through.

I wasn't honest about all this with Katherine. I simply told her, 'I'm not crazy about asking people for money, but I'd really like to go to Uganda.'

Katherine contacted her brother, who was now the US-based overseas director of the mission, and a few weeks later, he set up a three-way phone call between himself, me and Scott. Things happened quickly. I sent out letters to a small group of friends and the few thousand dollars I needed to raise began trickling in. I took this as a sign from God that going to Uganda was what He wanted me to do. When the trip seemed like it would really happen, I found a renter for my apartment. In the Bronx, I went through my files, packed up boxes and wept again, this time at my two send-off parties. I knew I had to leave and it was the right thing to do, but severing those relationships was far more painful than I'd anticipated.

That was five weeks ago now but seems far longer. Yet, here I am in Jennifer and Scott's living room recounting how I got to Bundibugyo. Learning about these background details, Scott recalls our first conversation.

'The phone reception wasn't great and it was about to rain so I had to cut the call short.'

'I remember thinking it was so strange that you were outside on the phone.'

'The signal here is pretty bad. You'll find that out soon enough,' Scott smiles. 'We're so glad you were willing to come. We knew we could use you to help us with Kwejuna.'

I have no way of knowing how true his words will turn out to be.

# 4
# The Health Centre

The following morning, I meet Jennifer outside the duplex, excited at the prospect of riding a bicycle. Using a second-hand one parked in the greeting room, and wearing a borrowed helmet, I find myself wobbling down the driveway, the sun's warmth on my face.

'Jennifer, this is tricky, riding in a dress.'

'Tuck the extra folds under you like I've done but keep them loose enough so you can pedal. You'll get used to it.'

She pulls ahead of me, lugging a black knapsack that looks heavier than mine, and turns left. Gripping the handlebars and with my dress flapping, I bounce along after her, dust swirling off the uneven surface which slopes downward. We pass a woman balancing firewood on her head and then two teenage boys in school uniforms gawk at us. Roadside dwellings, some made from cement, others from mud and sticks, slip by. Shrubs and eucalyptus trees are dotted between them. After several minutes, as the people and buildings increase, Jennifer points out a fenced compound with a mango tree towering in front of a gate. Behind it is a large field, and beyond that, a row of white single-storey buildings.

'There's Christ School and in to the right is RMS, Rwenzori Mission School, where our kids go.'

We soon pass the grounds and approach a fork. At the intersection, women gathered around a tap look up and stare.

Water gushes from the pump, filling up a well-worn yellow jerrycan arranged beside other containers of various sizes. Staying on the main road, lined with shops which are closed at this hour, I notice a brown two-storey dwelling called 'Nyahuka Holiday Inn'. We bike into a stretch of road, sandwiched between pick-up trucks and motorcycles. I smell exhaust and hear engines gunning. Twenty-something-looking men are loitering around. Heads turn and conversations stop as we pass.

'Jennifa!' someone calls out. She begins to get away from me. I pedal faster, scrambling to catch her. As I close the gap, Jennifer slows down and turns right, leading us through a narrow gate. A white sign announces that this is Nyahuka Health Centre. No driveway or car park is visible, though several motorcycles are standing idle. Inside, there's a narrow path leading to another open gate and a cluster of buildings beyond it. We dismount and walk our bikes towards them.

'Here's the lab and on the other side is the outpatient clinic.' Jennifer points to a grey structure. Patients, mostly women with young children, mill around. The atmosphere is subdued.

'What's this?' I ask, pointing to a free-standing building the size of a large garage.

'That's the operating theatre, but it's never used. There's no government doctor here, so there are no operations. Not even C-sections.'

'What happens if a woman needs one?'

'The midwives refer her to Bundibugyo Hospital, twelve kilometres away. Scott'll take you there on Friday. Some women don't make it in time.'

'Really?'

'Oftentimes there's a delay at the hospital when they get there. No fuel to run the generator, or the doctors demand money before they'll operate.'

'Is that legal?'

'Of course not, but it happens all the time. Most people can't afford to pay.' She shakes her head. 'We see a lot of that, people dying of things that are preventable.'

'What do you mean?'

'Well, if we had a doctor here at Nyahuka who could operate, some of that would change. We've helped to train a good friend of ours, Dr Jonah. He's in his final year of residency. You'd like him,' she says looking at me. I offer a tentative nod. 'He was a clinical officer when we first came but he had a dream of going to medical school. When we saw how good he was with patients, we decided to support him.' Then, almost as an afterthought she adds, 'He almost didn't make it.'

'Why not?'

'He did so well in the mature age entry exam, they thought he must've cheated.' She shakes her head. 'Because he was from Bundibugyo.'

'My goodness. Really?'

'They deleted his result and he had to take it again the next year.'

'No!'

'The second time around when he scored in the top three, they had to take him. This was at the top medical school in the country, Makerere University.'

'Bundibugyo's reputation is that bad?'

'Sad, isn't it? Jonah's in Kampala right now, like I said, in his final year of residency. When he's comes back, we're really hoping he'll get the operating theatre going.'

'When will he be back?'

'Next summer, hopefully.'

'What a shame I won't meet him.'

As we park our bikes under a covered walkway, Jennifer goes on to explain that the Ministry of Health manages all the health centres in Bundibugyo. There are no private facilities and no clinics run by *Médecins Sans Frontières* or other charities. Besides her and Scott, who raised funds in America for their salaries, there are only two other doctors in the district and they work at the hospital. The top job at Nyahuka is for a Ugandan, all the more reason they're eager for Dr Jonah to fill it.

When we get to the paediatric ward, Jennifer stops to retrieve a white lab coat and stethoscope from her knapsack. The ward is a grim open space with peeling paint and a foreboding smell of urine. I see a cluster of single beds, made of old metal frames and wiry springs, crammed with children and adults. With twice as many people as beds, many are sprawled on floor mats. An infant yells in a corner, tears sliding down its face.

'Families bring everything they'll need when they come here: mattresses, sheets, towels, soap,' Jennifer tells me. 'And they come here to stay because someone has to be here with these sick kids, to cook for them, feed them, wash their clothes. Change their bedding too.'

'Wow,' I say, shaking my head.

'It's a big deal to be hospitalised here.'

As we begin rounds, a young nurse, taller and darker than me, joins us. Our first stop is a baby a few months old, suffering from *kwashiorkor*, caused by a lack of protein. I recognise its signs from seeing it among poor children in Jos: matchstick limbs, a bloated stomach and orange-tinted hair. The tiny infant, buried in the arms of a mature woman, is suckling from a withered breast. Jennifer beams at them, greets the woman, and begins to ask her questions in the local language, Lubwisi. As they talk, Jennifer retrieves a thin blue exercise book from the edge of the bed.

Scanning its contents, Jennifer tells me, 'This is a *kitabo* and this woman here is the baby's grandmother, the father's mother. The baby's mother died several weeks after the baby was born. That's what's caused the malnutrition.'

I look intently at the woman, with a lined face and greying plaits, cradling the baby. 'This grandmother's breastfeeding her?'

Jennifer nods. 'Yes, it can happen. We don't know how old she is, probably about fifty. She had her own children years ago but when she came in, the nurses encouraged her to put the baby on her breasts. She was reluctant at first, but they kept urging her. The baby's suckling activated the milk hormones. Well, in this case, it reactivated them.'

'That's possible?' I ask, incredulous.

'The woman has to be really persistent and she and the baby have to bond. Her milk started coming in a few days ago and the baby's gaining weight.'

I look again at the scrawny infant and watch her tiny lips moving in rhythm, and for the second time in as many days, I tingle with excitement. I'm witnessing a miracle, life emerging from death.

Jennifer continues, 'It's too early to tell if the milk came in time to save the baby, but we hope so.' She scribbles something in the notebook, finds a sweet in her pocket and drops it into the hands of the grandmother. The woman responds with a broad grin missing most teeth. I can't help but join her.

Reluctantly, with me still beaming, we move on to the next bed. There, we find a young woman cradling a tiny, sickly baby.

'This little girl's not only malnourished but has TB,' Jennifer tells me. 'Though she's thirteen months, she's the size of a three-month-old.' I wince. She could be a poster child for a famine-relief fund-raiser. While talking to the patient's mother, Jennifer tries to coax a smile from the infant. Her faint lips respond with a hint of pleasure.

'I'm writing her mother a prescription. The health centre doesn't have these medications, so she'll have to buy them at a drug shop.'

'A drug shop?'

'Storefronts that serve as pharmacies. There are lots of them around. There's always a shortage of drugs at this health centre. Healthcare may be free, but most of the medicines aren't.'

The morning is a full one. Over the next few hours, we make our way through the dozen occupied beds squeezed into the ward, seeing children with malaria and sickle cell, others with TB, and more who are malnourished. When rounds are finished, we leave the nurse to follow up on dispensing medicines that the health centre has.

Jennifer and I walk over to the outpatient clinic. The waiting area is empty, but Jennifer wants to stop to talk with a lab tech at an office nearby. So, I find a bench and sit down, grateful for a few moments alone. After fishing around for my water bottle, I take a long drink, which is now lukewarm. My head is swimming. Even though I've just arrived, I can already see that being in Bundibugyo is going to expose me to far more than just HIV and AIDS. At the same time, along with public health, how I wish I also had clinical skills. They're so desperately needed here.

I close my eyes to relax and the next thing I know, I'm jerking awake. Bolting upright I look around, but see no one. I take another swig of water, hoping it will help, but I'm still sleepy. After a few more minutes of trying not to nod off, I see Jennifer approaching.

'I'm ready for lunch. You?' she asks.

'Yes! Jetlag's catching up with me as well,' I tell her, chuckling.

'You'll be able to rest after lunch.'

'Great.'

'We'll go back to our house, but on the way, I'll give you a quick tour of the mission.'

# 5
# The Team

The mission is a collection of buildings, mostly homes, dotted over a few acres along the main road. Cycling up from the health centre, we first come to the duplex where I'm staying, which shares a yard with another house. Set back behind a row of eucalyptus trees, but visible to passing vehicles and pedestrians, there is no fence or gate.

We turn right onto the property, bypass these houses and veer up a gradual incline. I realise I came this way yesterday when walking to dinner but now, in the daylight, I notice homes I'd not paid attention to then. Jennifer points out one that's empty, one which is for two single guys, and the other where Karen and her family live. Interspersed with these are the small cement dwellings of several Ugandan families, beside rows of tilled soil where maize, cabbage, tomatoes and cassava are growing.

'In front of us is the workshop and beyond that the community centre,' Jennifer explains when I draw alongside her. 'That's where the Kwejuna office is.' Cycling past, I hear the sound of a hammer and see two men kneeling over a bedframe. We follow the trail and pedal across the road to her home. She parks her bike in the shade. I lean mine against a wall. As we approach the house, her phone rings. The call is brief.

'That was Pat. She's going to join us for lunch.'

Pat is one of the main reasons I felt I could survive a stint in rural Uganda. Before I came here, I hadn't seen a photo of her or talked with her on the phone, but from follow-up conversations with Katherine, I knew there was an older single woman on the team. Pat came and settled in Uganda in her late thirties, and like me, Pat was not married nor did she have children. When I was preparing to spend these months in Uganda, I was mindful that I would be arriving with neither a husband nor a child. For African women, both of these – but especially being a mother – are markers of womanhood, so I was especially self-conscious about being childless.

Instead, in my early thirties I had given birth to a PhD in sociomedical sciences, a branch of public health, at Columbia University, the first African-born woman to do so. This degree meant I was called 'Doctor' in professional circles in New York City, but in this under-resourced setting where medical doctors are sorely needed, I'm unable to provide clinical care. While I'd thought about this before I got here and it came up again seeing all those patients at the clinic this morning, it was not having children at my age that I was more concerned about. That Pat had helped local people to understand that women who aren't from here don't always marry nor have children was significant. It meant I could appear less odd than I felt.

While Jennifer and I are having a drink of water in her kitchen, we hear a vehicle pull up. Outside, there's a navy Nissan Patrol, identical to the one I rode in from the airstrip, except this one is dusty and stuffed full of trunks and boxes. Pat is climbing out of what appears to be the passenger side, but then I remember that the steering wheel is on the 'wrong' side since they drive on the left in Uganda, like they do in the UK. Pat is shorter than me, has a henna-highlighted bob and looks younger than her late forties would suggest.

'Pamela, it's wonderful to meet you.' She holds on to me like a long-lost friend.

'How was the ride?' Jennifer asks her.

'Fine, thanks be to God. Hey, look what I brought you.' Ducking into the back seat, Pat retrieves a basket brimming with lettuce, broccoli and carrots.

'Thanks. We can always do with more veggies.'

Over lunch, I discover Pat is spunky and has a *joie de vivre* about her. She also seems to have the knack of making each person she's speaking to feel as if they're the only one that counts. Later, after helping her unpack her car, I spend the afternoon resting and watching my new housemate receive a steady stream of Ugandans welcoming her back as if she's been gone for months, rather than a week.

I go back to Nyahuka Health Centre the next day, this time with Scott for his weekly ultrasound clinic. He performs scans on HIV-positive pregnant mothers to check the health of the foetus and confirm the baby's due date. Sometimes the midwives also refer high-risk patients who don't have HIV. Today there are five women, three of whom are HIV-negative.

'This woman's thirty and this is her eighth pregnancy,' Scott tells me. Stunning, with high cheekbones and flawless charcoal skin, it's hard to believe she's had seven children. On the exam table, she lifts up her top exposing a small round bump around her middle. Scott rubs gel on it and runs the probe from the portable machine up and down and around and over. I look at the small screen, a blur of greys and whites and blacks.

'There's no baby,' he says to me, his voice low.

'Really?' I peer at the screen again but see nothing distinctive. Scott turns to the woman and speaks to her in Lubwisi. At first, she registers no reaction and then she sits up slowly shaking her head. Her eyes filling with tears, she pulls her rainbow-coloured shawl over her shoulders, slides off the table, and is gone.

'What happened?' I ask.

'Looks like she miscarried.' I press my lips together and shake my head.

The next woman enters. She has an overgrown afro and is wearing a shiny locket around her neck. During her scan, Scott points out two heartbeats on the monitor, a blur of grey, popping up and down like the sound of a flat tyre on a rough road. He tells the woman she's carrying twins. Her facial expression doesn't change. Same for the third woman when Scott confirms her due date as Valentine's Day. He confirms the dates for the other two who are HIV-positive as well. There are no smiles, no hint of joy from any of them. After their scans, they wipe off the gel, rearrange their tops and step outside.

'Scott, aren't these women happy to be pregnant? What's going on?'

'It's common for them not to show any emotions. Doesn't mean they aren't happy, but unlike in America, women here don't buy soap or clothes or anything for the baby until it's been born and they know it's survived.'

'Is that because of miscarriages?'

'Not just that. Children can die in childbirth too, and it's riskier if they're born at home. Because families are so poor, they don't spend money on baby things until they're sure they have to.'

My heart aches for these women, but I say nothing more as Scott packs up his machine and we head outside.

'Alex!'

Looking in the direction Scott's calling, I see a man cycling through the gates. He makes a detour and rides towards us. His polished black shoes, button-down shirt and dark slacks catch my eye, making him the best-dressed person I've seen here so far. If he weren't riding a bicycle with large black bags balancing precariously on the back, I'd think he were heading to an enviable city job.

'Alex, how are you? Taking mama kits to the labour ward?'

'Am fine, doctor. Yes, am going there now.' Alex looks in my direction, a distant expression in his eyes.

'This is Dr Pamela, here to help us with the Kwejuna Project.'

I extend my hand. Alex's handshake is not very convincing.

'Alex is the administrative assistant for Kwejuna at Nyahuka,' Scott says, introducing Alex, before turning back to him. 'How many do you have?'

'Fifty.'

'Very good.' Scott smiles.

As Alex cycles away, Scott explains that mama kits are bags of supplies given to the midwives to ensure a safe delivery for each pregnant woman. He goes on to tell me, 'Alex is from Kasese, a nearby district more developed than Bundibugyo. They have electricity and some paved roads.' Perhaps that explains his outfit, I muse to myself. 'It's even hotter than here 'cause it's closer to the equator.'

'How did Alex end up working with Kwejuna?'

'Not sure why he first came to Bundibugyo, but he was one of the community mobilisers I hired when we were getting started.'

'You hired people to get the community involved?' I'm both surprised and pleased.

'Yeah, we needed to let them know what Kwejuna was all about. Alex did a great job organising a drama group. Helped us get village mayors on board too, so I brought him on full-time. I really wanted to hire women for Kwejuna but couldn't find them.' Scott's voice trails off.

'What do you mean?'

'Well, men are more educated here and Alex had done so well. But now…' Scott scratches his cheek. 'Am not so sure he's right for the job. It's only a hunch, but I hope I'm wrong.'

The following afternoon, we assemble as a team, a weekly event that happens in Scott and Jennifer's living room. Live geckoes scampering up into the ceiling have replaced the dancing shadows of three nights ago. They make me jittery, so I avoid looking at them and glance instead around the room. It's the first time I'm seeing everyone together in the same place. Scott opens the meeting by introducing me.

'We're pleased to have Dr Pamela –' he says.

'Just Pamela is OK,' I say, speaking over him.

'She's here with us until the end of January,' he continues.

Smiles welcome me. I plant a grin on my face, appearing braver than I feel. My new community consists of two families plus a married couple, a husband whose wife is in the US awaiting the birth of twins, and a handful of single people who have welcomed me as one of them. Still, I'm aware of our differences: I'm a short-term volunteer, not a missionary, and the only non-American, who has roots in urban Africa, a Nigerian passport and brown skin.

After a time of Bible study, discussion and prayer, we adjourn outdoors to share a meal of pizza. Scott, who evidently built the brick oven some years back, takes over as the chef. Gloves and metal spatula in hand, he peers into it to check the furnace which has been going all afternoon. I lean in as he turns the coals, red-hot and roaring, a gust of heat blasting in my face.

'Pamela, you'll need to be careful of no-see-ums at this time of day,' Pat warns as I jerk back from the scorching oven. Katherine had warned me about these too.

'Are they really called no-see-ums?'

'Yes, they're tiny and hard to see but they love blood and will find it if you leave any skin uncovered.' I put on a baseball cap I've brought in my bag and pull a long-sleeved shirt over my top. 'Here, use this as well,' Pat says, handing me a bottle of insect repellent. I hate being bitten, so despite the balmy temperature, I smother my hands, neck and ears with the sticky spray. The smell reminds me of dousing our bedrooms in Jos just before sleeping, to ward off hungry mosquitoes. The kids have scattered, squealing as they run around the yard chasing each other. The rest of us hang around close to the oven, drinking sodas and beer and chatting. Jennifer, Karen and Bethany have covered up with aprons and are flattening balls of dough into bases for the pizza.

'Have you ever made pizza from scratch before?' Pat asks. I shake my head. 'You want to try rolling the dough?'

'Uh, not today. Perhaps next time.' I've had my fill of novel experiences for now. Besides I'm feeling a bit conflicted about making pizza in this resource-limited out-of-the-way place. Shouldn't we be sampling local food instead?

Within minutes, the first pizzas are ready, the mozzarella on top still sizzling. Leaving the others, Pat and I sit under the bougainvillea-covered trellis. The sun, the colour of a ripe mango, is falling in the west. The sky is a fiery glow of pinks and oranges. The top of my left ear itches where a no-see-um has found an uncovered spot and bitten me. I scratch it but the itch intensifies. Ignoring my discomfort, I sink my teeth into a slice. The base is thin and firm but not overcooked. The cheese is soft and chewy.

'This is delicious. I can't believe I'm eating pizza here, of all places.'

'Awesome, isn't it?' says Pat. Not wanting to venture into a heavy conversation about pizza and poverty, I decide to keep things light-hearted.

'So,' I ask her, 'how did you end up coming to live here?'

'Well, I was thirty-six and working as a waitress in Winston-Salem. I made ice cream and sandwiches in a coffee shop, but the truth was, I didn't have much direction. When a pastor at my church suggested I come to Bundibugyo, I thought, "Why not?"' She says these last two words with a thick British-Ugandan accent.

'Had you ever been to Africa before?'

'I'd never been out of the States before. I didn't even have a passport.'

'Really?' I ask in disbelief. 'What a big step.'

'It was. When I first came here, I taught two little kids. They wanted me to teach Katherine's niece and nephew as well, but I couldn't manage all four.' Laughing she adds, 'They're teenagers now, in Philadelphia. After that year, they asked me to join the team.'

'Did you keep teaching?'

'No, I spent a year learning Lubwisi. Soon I was leading women's Bible studies. Recently I've been helping at the nutrition clinic. Then when Kwejuna began, Scott asked me to lead a support group at Nyahuka. I hope to start another one at the hospital too.'

Jennifer has come over while Pat is speaking. She adds to the story.

'Pat's the one with the most friendships here. She's got great Lubwisi and she really goes out of her way to love people. Bakes wedding cakes, sponsors kids in school, helps families at funerals, and even drives pregnant women to Bundibugyo Hospital.'

'I love doing all of those things. Doesn't mean it isn't hard, though, too. People here have so many needs. Sometimes it feels like we're not making much difference.'

'True,' says Jennifer. 'Hey, I came to see if either of you want any more pizza. Grab it before we start cleaning up.'

'Want some more?' asks Pat, turning to me.

'Why not?' I ask, imitating her Ugandan English. Pat throws her head back and laughs. After eating another slice, we help to tidy up by tossing out half-eaten crusts and throwing dirty plates into a purple basin filling with water at an outside tap. As we haul chairs back into the sitting room, I catch myself in a yawn and try to stifle it.

'Want to stay for the movie?' Pat asks.

'There's a movie? Now?'

'Yes, after pizza we usually watch a movie. Scott puts up a sheet and projects a DVD onto it.'

I shake my head. 'Sounds like fun, but I don't have the energy for that. I'm going to head back.'

Later, as I settle under the covers, my mind savours the highlights of the past four days: that spectacular flight in over the mountains, the stunning beauty of this place, and the grandmother whose shrunken breasts are nursing her granddaughter back from death. Then there are also the pregnant women who dare not rejoice when they see their unborn babies' beating hearts, the dearth of doctors and the lack of drugs.

Like the Africa I know from Nigeria, Bundibugyo seems to be a place of deep contradictions; yet I want to see and experience all I can. I'm especially eager to connect more with Ugandans. I hope that will come tomorrow when I visit the hospital with Scott to observe the Kwejuna Project in action.

# 6
# The News

Scott's red Land Rover fills the centre of the road, elephant grass on either side. Rounding a corner, we meet a battered Toyota pick-up taxi. We lurch over to the left and then veer back to the middle once we've passed it. Careening up modest hills and down again over a surface lacerated with small stones and deep rifts, the jeep bounces in a jarring rhythm, making me wonder if I'll ever get used to it.

I look over at Scott. His eyes are fixed ahead. Resting his right elbow in the open window while steering with this same hand, he appears casual but confident. He's seemed pensive this morning so, taking his lead, I've kept quiet. Now, as if Scott senses that I'm watching him, he looks over at me and begins to open up.

'Let me tell you about our kids.' He gives me a brief history. While it hasn't been easy, all of them have developed a deep sense of connection to this beautiful place. Luke, their oldest, will start at Christ School next year.

'It's for boarders, but since it's so close, he'll live at home. He's the most well-adjusted of our kids. We think he's ready for the challenge.'

I realise what a big step this is. 'He'll be the only white student, right?'

'Yes, the only *muzungu*, but we think he'll be OK. He's made some good Ugandan friends who'll be going there too.'

Scott looks at me again, pursing his lips before continuing.

'When we spoke on the phone before you came, I told you Bundibugyo is home for us. I also told you we always spend Christmas here.' He pauses.

I've been curious about what it will be like to be in Bundibugyo for Christmas. Several months ago, I never would have guessed this is where I'd spend that holiday.

Scott hesitates and then goes on. 'Last night we got a call from Jennifer's parents. Her dad has been having some troubling symptoms – difficulty walking at times and episodes of slurred speech. We encouraged him to get a full check-up.'

I murmur in response, not sure where this conversation is headed. I look at him, confused.

Scott keeps his focus up ahead. 'The results just came back.'

I fix my eyes on his profile.

'He's been diagnosed with ALS. It's a degenerative neuromuscular condition. You may know it as Lou Gehrig's or motor neurone disease.'

Despite my training in public health, I know little about this, and have never known anyone with it.

'What are the symptoms?'

'Progressive muscle deterioration,' he tells me, still concentrating on the road. 'He'll get to the point where he won't be able to speak. He won't be able eat on his own or breathe without a respirator. His mind won't be affected, but his body will gradually break down.'

'Is there any treatment?' I ask, not sure why he's sharing all of this with me.

'There are some drugs to slow the muscle loss, but there's no cure.' Scott swallows hard.

I wait for him to speak again, still puzzled about what this means.

'He may only have about a year or so to live.' Saying this, he turns to look at me. Pale blue eyes peer out through his glasses and meet mine. I stare back through my own specs.

'I'm so sorry.'

Then, turning back to the road, he drops the bombshell.

'We've decided to spend Christmas in the States.' He waits before continuing. I keep staring at him. 'It may be his last one.' He's quiet again. 'I called this morning and was able to get us on a flight in early December. We'll leave right after the ambassador's visit.'

I feel a lump forming in my throat.

I say nothing but am struck by how quickly they've made their plans. Focusing on the ruts in the road, I try to stop my mind from darting all over the place. It's nearly impossible to control my thoughts, so I keep replaying what I've just learned. Scott and Jennifer, who I came here to work with four days ago, will be leaving, in a month.

I wonder what this will mean for me. Will I have to leave too? That would be ridiculous, wouldn't it? After all, I've made a three-month commitment and it's not as if I'm here by myself. There's a team, though none of the others, except Pat, work with the AIDS programme. Scott accelerates up a steep stretch of road, wrapped around the side of a mountain like a banana fibre binding the rim of a basket. As we reach the edge of town at the top of that prolonged hill, my thoughts swirling, my tummy doing somersaults, I pray that I've not exchanged one stress-filled job for another.

Bundibugyo Town, with a population of 50,000 and the only town to speak of here, is the district capital. The hospital, just inside the city limits, lies along the main road, and has the mountains as a backdrop. Scott parks under a mango tree near pink hibiscus flowers blooming in front of a single-storey building. Besides a motorcycle, the only other vehicle there is a dusty white pick-up-turned-ambulance, its front tyre in need of repair.

Walking along a series of covered walkways, Scott gives me a cursory tour. We wander through the outpatient department. An open-air waiting area thronged with sick people, it smells like a combination of sores and disinfectant. We pass by the operating theatre. Scott tells me the two doctors who work here perform minor surgeries only when there's fuel for the generator to sterilise equipment and provide adequate lighting. Thus, lots of deaths happen which could be prevented. A similar sad story to the one Jennifer told me at Nyahuka.

We soon come to the inpatient building and as we enter it, I notice a laminated sign affixed to the door. Outlined in black on a white background is a logo of an African woman with a baby on her back, reaching down to a small girl whose arms are extended up towards her. The notice announces Scott and Jennifer's HIV prevention programme, Kwejuna.

\* \* \*

In September 2003, fourteen months before I arrived in Bundibugyo, the prestigious scientific journal *The Lancet* published the results of a landmark study. Researchers had identified a simple way of preventing mother-to-child transmission of HIV: a single dose of nevirapine, an antiretroviral drug, given to mothers during labour and to newborns – within three days of their birth – cut in half the chance that a baby would be born with HIV.[1] The study had taken place in Kampala and scientists from the same research network our Bronx studies were a part of had conducted the work.

Fortunately, most babies born to a mother with HIV will not become infected. But without medical intervention, up to a third of babies will acquire the virus, either during pregnancy, at birth, or through breastfeeding. In developed countries, offering Caesarean sections, treating infected mothers with drugs and eliminating breastfeeding have meant that the risk of passing HIV from the mother to her baby has all but been eliminated. However, in settings like Bundibugyo where these options are not possible or realistic, the single dose approach can save the lives of some babies who would otherwise become infected.[2]

It's a thrill for me to be working on HIV prevention in this country, because Uganda was *the* African AIDS success story at the start of the new millennium. Unlike so many other African countries struggling to contain the spread of the virus, HIV prevalence rates dropped among pregnant women in Uganda from one in five (21 per cent) in 1991 to one in twenty (6 per cent) in 2001.[3] This dramatic decline was the result of wide-reaching AIDS awareness efforts that President Yoweri Museveni, who came to power in 1986, spearheaded. Known as the ABC approach, 'A' was for 'Abstain from sex before marriage', 'B' was for 'Be faithful to one partner' and 'C' was for 'use a Condom' if abstinence and fidelity are not possible. Whether it's the 'A', the 'B', the 'C' or some combination that has had the greatest impact in reducing HIV rates remains a source of much contention.[4]

However, despite the success of HIV/AIDS prevention efforts throughout Uganda in the nineties, there was not a single AIDS programme implemented in Bundibugyo. That changed when the US-based Elizabeth Glaser Pediatric AIDS Foundation (EGPAF) awarded a grant to Scott and Jennifer to establish an HIV prevention programme for pregnant mothers and their babies. They called it Kwejuna, an ingenious name, taken from the greeting women receive when they've had a baby. *'Weebale Kwejuna'* literally means 'thank you for helping yourself out of that problem'.

\* \* \*

I follow Scott past the door with the Kwejuna logo of the mother and children. At the end of a dim corridor, we enter a room that's bare except for a cluttered desk, a wooden chair and a cheerful man who quickly stands as we enter. Scott introduces me to Joseph, Kwejuna's hospital-based administrative assistant. Babwisi by tribe, Joseph is stocky, looks about thirty, and is a little over five feet, typical for adult males here due to generations of chronic malnutrition. Wearing a yellow T-shirt with the same logo we just saw, he extends his hand and greets me warmly, exposing rows of white teeth. I take to him immediately.

'How many women are here today?' Scott asks Joseph.

'The same as every Friday, about fifty so far, but they are still registering them.' Turning to me, he adds, 'We can get eighty or even ninety who come for their first prenatal visit. Can I show you the clinic?'

Joseph leads us next door to a large room at the end of the hall thronged with young women, their stomachs swollen to different sizes. They sit crammed together on rows of hard benches, many with little ones playing or crying. They're listening, or trying to listen, to a woman facing them who appears to be conducting a health education session.

Our entrance causes a distraction. The woman, brown like cocoa and with straightened hair, stops and then beams when she sees Scott. We walk over to her. Scott says hello to the midwife and then speaks to the sea of faces in front of us using a greeting in Lubwisi. The women respond in unison like a choir but with grins and chuckles. I wonder if they're amused by his accent. When Scott introduces me to them, I feel sixty pairs of eyes staring. I blink back, wondering what they're thinking, speculating about what they see when they look at this latest visitor. My eyes sweep across the group as perspiration breaks out on my forehead. I want to reveal our shared African heritage, want to open my mouth and try to say something that will connect me to them, but I can't. Besides, the gulf between us is a chasm which extends far beyond the language barrier. My years of living in the US, my socioeconomic advantages and mixed-race heritage have conspired to construct differences. I nod and plant a big smile on my face. The moment passes and the midwife continues teaching. We move on.

'She's doing HIV counselling,' Scott tells me. 'After counselling, they'll all be tested. The ones who're positive will be told and get a dose of nevirapine to take home for when labour starts. Nevirapine syrup's here at the hospital for their newborns. The midwives try to persuade these mothers to come back here to give birth, but most moms still deliver at home.'

Joseph explains a bit more: 'When the midwife is finished, the women will go for testing to the lab.' He nods in the direction of a hallway. 'It doesn't take long, about twenty minutes.'

'On any given day, how many women test positive?' I ask.

'It depends. Sometimes one or two.'

'Do they understand what it means?'

'Many people know Slim, that's what we call it here. But they think Slim is only when you're very sick and not eating. For these women, who look healthy, it's difficult for them to believe they have the virus. Even if they believe, when they go home, they won't tell anybody.'

'Not even their husband?' I ask.

'Especially the husband. He could leave them and take the children.'

Scott explains, 'Children belong to the father here. For the women today who'll be finding out they have HIV, of course it's devastating news. On the other hand, we've been surprised and relieved that HIV infection rates aren't much higher.'

'What are they?'

'Well, between the hospital and Nyahuka, about 3 per cent of the women we're testing are positive. Less than half the national average of 7.5 per cent for pregnant women.'

'That's really encouraging. Why do you think it's so low?'

'Probably because Bundibugyo is so remote. The mountains and the poor road have helped to limit the virus from making its way here from Kampala and the other big cities.'

'We have a Kwejuna mother here now,' Joseph tells us. 'She delivered yesterday. Want to see her?' he asks.

We shuffle out of the office and make our way to the maternity ward, another drab building across the walkway from the prenatal clinic. Entering the main hall, Joseph points out one of the private rooms. Scott approaches the door, knocks and we enter. The space is poky, the walls a dingy two-tone teal and white. The sole piece of furniture is a single bed, where a woman, probably in her early twenties, with thick braids, is seated. She's clutching a bundle of lace. A rail-thin man is wedged beside her.

The young couple look up, their faces breaking into tentative smiles when they see us. The man, wearing a tailored shirt and slacks, rises as Scott approaches the new mother.

'*Weebale Kwejuna*,' he says to her.

'*Weebale kusaba*,' she replies, thanking him and beaming.

'How are the babies doing?'

It's only when Scott asks this that I notice a second bundle on the bed, wrapped in the same lace cloth the woman is holding.

'Fine, doctah,' the man replies.

'They were delivered yesterday?'

'Yes, doctah.'

'They got nevirapine?'

'Yes, doctah.'

'It's very good you came to the hospital.'

'Thank you, doctah.'

'When do you leave?'

'We are leaving tomorrow, to go to Kasese. My barracks are there.'

'Ah, you are a soldier. Will you take your wife and children with you?'

'Yes, doctah.'

Scott reaches over the bed to examine each twin. I lean forward to watch. Pulling back the layers they're wrapped in, we discover one is a girl, the other a boy. Their perfectly formed hands are curled into tight fists like boxers as if they're anticipating what's to come.

I can't help but wonder about all that lies ahead for these beautiful babies. Because they're twins, they'll compete for resources that would otherwise go to one child. And this couple won't have the support they'd receive if they were living close to family. Both parents look healthy now, but how much time do they have before this virus begins to take over their lives?

Not a promising start for them.

Not an encouraging start for me either.

Seeing these newborns takes me back to my conversation with Scott in the Land Rover.

'We'll be away for six weeks over Christmas and New Year,' he told me. 'Back at the end of January. For the retreat in Jinja.' He sounded so matter of fact. I came knowing I would leave right after that retreat. Hearing him lay out this new plan, I realised once they left in December, I wouldn't see them again in Bundibugyo. My ribcage got tight.

As if that wasn't unsettling enough, there was more.

'While we're away, I'd like you to become the acting director of Kwejuna,' Scott said.

'Really?' I asked, fighting to steady my voice even as the muscles in my shoulders began to protest. I didn't sign up for this.

He went on, 'You bring a lot of experience from what you've done in New York, and you'll be working closely with Joseph and Alex. They know the programme well.'

I remained quiet, confused, doubtful even, but my insides were churning. When I left the Bronx and decided to come here, the last thing I expected was to find myself in a leadership position. I'd had enough and was more than ready to give up all of the responsibilities that come with that sort of role. I leapt on board with what sounded like an exciting adventure and thought my desire to work in Africa would trump any trials I might face. Coming to an unknown place and working with people I didn't know would have its challenges, sure, but I knew God would be with me and I was familiar with this part of the world, Nigeria at least. And someone else would be in charge. At least that's what I thought.

As we thank the soldier and his wife, I'm aware the twins are two children I won't be tracking down. I came to Bundibugyo to look for lost HIV-positive women and to check up on their newborns. And now, here on my first day of encountering the Kwejuna Project, I'm learning my scope will be much broader.

This news about Scott and his family leaving has shaken me. Despite my best efforts at self-control, I can't help myself from thinking about all that'll soon change. Though I tend to have a delayed emotional reaction to hard things, eventually the intensity of my feelings catches up. Now that I've had more than an hour for this shifting situation to sink in, my anxiety is mounting. A knot has congealed in my stomach and I'm perspiring under my dress. I fear becoming overwhelmed, or worse, letting Scott or the programme down. But I keep trying to remind myself that the reality is I'm in a place where the needs are vast and life is harsh. I believe God brought me here to help and I recognise that a life with God often (always?) means He'll lead us where we wouldn't choose to go.

On our way back to the mission, tugging at the fabric clinging to my waist to let in some air, I stare out of the window. My eyes scan the hillsides, the dips in the valleys and the swell of the mountains. The beauty signals God's presence and reminds me how fortunate I am to be living in such a spectacular location. But the truth is, I'm glad I'll only be here for a few months. I just got here and life in Bundibugyo is already proving to be a bit too unpredictable.

By the time Scott pulls up in front of his house, I try to push my anxiety away by pretending it's not there. Looking ahead to what I'll be doing next week, I focus my thoughts on going out to look for lost Kwejuna mothers.

# 7
# The First Ride

I'm feeling unsettled. Diarrhoea has sent me to the pit latrine twice already this morning. Before I came here, getting on a motorcycle to look for HIV-infected women in the Ugandan countryside sounded adventurous. I envisioned myself criss-crossing the foothills of the Rwenzoris dispensing AIDS education and saving babies, but now that I'm about to ride one of these machines, I'm not feeling so brave. My first and only experience on a motorcycle was a two-minute spin around our yard thirty years ago, and I was terrified.

I try to quash these thoughts and downplay my queasy feelings as I head out to meet up with Masika, my translator. Though it's only nine, the equatorial sun is already scorching. My glasses are sliding and I keep having to push them back onto my nose. In ten minutes, I arrive at Masika's hair salon on the edge of the market. After we exchange greetings, she announces, 'Pam.Ella. Come, I'm taking you to the stage.' She begins to lead me through a maze of stalls, most not open yet.

'Stage?' I ask, perplexed as we pass a row of women lining up bottles of palm oil, the rich orange colour and pungent odour unmistakable.

'The stage,' Masika tells me, 'is where we get the *boda boda*. Where are we going?'

'A place called Busunga, to look for two women. You know Busunga?'

'I know it. It's near Congo. One *boda boda* or two?'

I hesitate and then blurt out, 'I think we should take two.'

Masika nods. 'It's OK.'

Most motorcycles carry multiple passengers here, but I'm not ready to be squeezed onto the back of a motorcycle with anyone besides the driver, even if it's Masika. I met her for the first time two days ago when she came to the duplex, offering to be my translator. Unlike most women here, she's lived outside Bundibugyo and learned English while attending secondary school in Kampala. She runs her own hair business, but it's seasonal, she'd explained. In these last two months of the year during cocoa harvesting, money flows and she does well. But once the season is over, finances become a struggle again. Hence, her eagerness to earn something extra even when the demand for hair care is high. Self-assured, with smooth coal-black skin and pressed hair, I like her logic and her eagerness to work.

When we reach the main road, Masika tells me to wait beside a locked shop a few doors down from a wide, unmarked area where several weary-looking Toyota pick-up trucks are parked.

'If the drivers see you are *muzungu,* they will add to the price,' she tells me, chuckling. Yes, I'm familiar with that scenario from market shopping in Jos. Hanging back, I sit on a step and try to look inconspicuous. I also try not to inhale the exhaust coming from the gunning of nearby motorcycle engines. Smoke from a fire where pancakes are frying uncoils into the air. My nose twitches. Athletic young men are mounted on their metal horses, eating breakfast and cracking jokes as they wait for their next fare. Into this mix, motorcycles arrive and people slide off them while others get on and leave, giving their drivers another excuse to rev their machines.

During breaks in this show of bravado, I overhear Masika, her voice alternating between speech and laughter. She eventually signals to me to approach. While she's explaining to me what's been agreed, our drivers purchase petrol stored in grimy water bottles sitting on the road's edge. Watching them dump the orange fuel into their tanks, I shudder, trying not to think about all the dirt that may be in those containers.

Fumes linger in the air as Masika introduces me to Desmond, my driver. Probably around thirty, he looks older due to his closely cropped hair and a receding hairline. He kickstarts his *boda boda* and following several attempts, it comes alive. This is my cue. I glance around for Masika. She's already hopped on, her hands gripping the waist of her driver. About twenty-something, he has a sea of milky white above the right side of his lip. Despite the colour, its appearance brings to mind Kaposi's sarcoma, the skin cancer that leaves telltale purple lesions, which was often seen on gay men in the US living with AIDS in the 1980s.

Trying to downplay the strange resemblance, I sidle up to Desmond's silver machine that is now growling softly. I feign nonchalance, plant my left foot, and begin to climb on. Gathering the folds of my dress, I swing my other leg around the wide black leather seat, hoping the fullness of the material hides what's underneath. A dozen *boda boda* drivers are hanging around. I sense they've been watching our every move. That other time on a motorcycle, I was ten, when an adult friend, showing off her new moped, took me for a ride. I was afraid then too, and like now, tried to hide it. Concentrating, I balance my bodyweight and before I know it, we are off.

As we whizz out of Nyahuka in a direction I've not been before, I cling to the rack behind. We lurch along the main road covered with deep furrows laced with small stones. Without a helmet, the wind whips my face; fortunately, my glasses shield my eyes. I notice a river up ahead at the base of a shallow valley. This section dips down, goes over a bridge and up a near vertical hill. As we descend, in a blur, I see women washing clothes in the water below, together with naked children frolicking beside them. I hold on tighter.

Desmond steers the machine up the steep incline, grinding the *boda boda* into a low gear. I clamp my eyes shut. We edge forward. After what feels like five minutes but is probably less than twenty seconds, we reach the top of the hill.

I open my eyes.

Like on my ride to the hospital with Scott, the road gives way to tall grass, banana trees and shrubs. We fly past clusters of huts, some glistening with zinc roofs, others with thatched tops. We pass a school. Boys are playing football in the field; girls are gathered under a mango tree. '*Muzungu!*' they call out when they spot me. Their voices soon fade. Snaking through the centre of a village, people stare. I pretend I don't see them looking. Later, we come to a shallow river and dismount. While the drivers wade across it with their motorcycles, we use a footbridge.

Getting back on the *boda bodas*, after twenty minutes, we reach Busunga. It appears to be just a cluster of huts. As we alight, a thin man approaches us, ragged salt-and-pepper strands hanging from his chin. His faded black slacks look like they lost their zipper long ago and are fastened together with safety pins. We learn he's the vice-chairman, an elected village official. There are no addresses here, but Masika gives him the names of the women we're looking for, explaining that we want to find out how their babies are doing. It's the truth but not all of it.

Satisfied with our explanation and confident he knows where they live, he becomes our guide. Leaving the motorcycles behind, we follow him. Navigating the terrain in a pair of worn flip-flops, he leads us past rice paddies and cocoa farms dotted with more banana trees. Those first huts have given way to countless others along an intricate array of paths. Like the many who farm here for a living, he's extremely fit. Masika and I struggle to keep up. When my pace slows, I hear her panting, steps behind me.

I'm in awe of this trek into rural life. The terrain continues to stun me. I don't know where we're going and would certainly be lost if I were on my own. I'm also struck by how far these women must have come to get to the health centre while they were pregnant. No wonder so many of them don't return when they're due to give birth.

After half an hour of following him and being winded, the vice-chairman slows down as we reach a clearing with more huts. He heads towards one where several women are sweeping in front. A little girl plays nearby. A man sits under a tree eating something that looks like porridge. He gets up as we approach. The women interrupt their work and stand upright. One by one, they greet the vice-chairman and he begins talking with them. As he's speaking, the three adults turn and stare at us. Then the younger woman, who has narrow braids that meet on the top of her head, smiles and nods.

I surmise she must be Zaituni, who we're looking for. Going into a hut, she returns with a bench, puts it down out of earshot, and retrieves a small stool for herself. Leaving the men to talk under the tree, we three women sit. Masika greets her in Lubwisi. I copy what Masika has said. A grin spreads across the young woman's face. She looks me in the eye without reservation. Masika lowers her voice, explaining that we're from Nyahuka Health Centre and are here to find out when she had her baby. She points to her daughter playing in the dirt near us – a toddler in a torn and faded pink dress. We ask her age. She's eighteen months.

I take out my clipboard and glance at my spreadsheet. Something doesn't fit. This can't be the child Zaituni was carrying when she came to the clinic in February. But her details and even the name of her husband, who's the man sitting under the tree with the vice-chairman, all match. Confused, I get Masika to ask whether she's had another baby since the toddler. She denies that. I watch her intently, willing her face to tell us if there's more to her story. Her expression gives nothing away. I check my records a second time. If they're accurate, she should have a baby a few weeks old. Either she does and she's not telling us, or more likely, the baby didn't survive. With no baby, there's not much to our visit. We thank her and move on.

The disappearance of Zaituni's baby puzzles me. I can't believe she'd deny the existence of a child she'd carried for nine months and pushed out alive even if it had then died. Or would she? I recall Scott's explanation for why the women getting sonograms didn't smile when they saw their babies in their wombs. Wondering if there's a data error in our register, which might explain the discrepancy, I make a note to verify it when I'm back at the Kwejuna office.

The vice-chairman again leads the way, weaving through a different array of paths and past more banana trees and cocoa fields. I tug on my nylon slip clinging to my thighs, trying to let in some air. We reach another clearing dotted with huts. A river hums nearby. I daub my face with a tissue before taking a drink of water. It's so warm, it doesn't do much for my thirst.

Our guide calls out to two boys playing nearby. They point us to a home, and as we approach, a young woman emerges holding a baby. She can't be more than sixteen. Her face is full, framed with a cropped head of hair. The vice-chairman asks her a question. She nods, looks at me and Masika, her eyebrows raised, and directs us to two benches under a tree. We sit and greet.

Masika tells her who we are and why we've come. The teenager responds with fear in her eyes and her jaw tightens. She confirms this is her first child. Wearing only a loose cloth, he's a beautiful four-month-old with a head of large, soft curls. He gazes at me with penetrating eyes. I ask to hold him. As soon as I take him in my arms, he pees all over my dress. Masika and I laugh, but his mother's expression remains serious. When we ask about her husband, she tells us he's a soldier but now gone. It's not clear if he ever met his son.

She says she wasn't given nevirapine at her visit. Thus, she had no reason to bring her baby to the health centre to receive his dose. It's possible the midwife didn't tell her she had HIV or didn't send her home with the pill. She was tested early on when the programme had just begun. Care was a bit patchy then. Or, she may be reluctant to admit she got the pill but never took it, for fear we will shame her. Whatever her situation, we can only speculate. Before we leave, she reluctantly agrees to pose for a photo, her eyes still filled with fright.

The glimmer of hope in her story is that her baby is probably not infected, given the odds. But there's the risk through breast milk. No pills can reduce that chance. She confirms she's nursing her son. His HIV risk will increase when she starts giving him solid foods along with her milk – which happens when babies are six months old – because solids can damage the intestinal lining, thereby facilitating HIV transmission. We encourage her to wean him quickly and urge her to bring him to the health centre for his routine childhood vaccinations.

With a slower pace, Masika and I make our way back to the motorcycles. I keep thinking about the young mother we just met. I have no idea what it's like to be facing the future that she's walking into. She seemed so vulnerable. I pray she has support for her own health situation and to help her raise her son. I also hope her son doesn't already have HIV. His status can't be confirmed for another eighteen months, when all her antibodies have cleared out of his blood. What a daunting set of circumstances, for any woman, let alone a sixteen-year-old.

When we reach our drivers, though sweaty and out of breath, I'm still sobered by this first outreach excursion, and relieved to be less nervous about getting back on.

# 8

# The Losses

I keep thinking about Zaituni's missing baby. Perhaps our data about her is inaccurate. Later that week, I go in search of the Kwejuna office at the health centre. I find it at the back of the waiting room in the clinic building, a crude wooden structure with a zinc roof. When I unlatch the door, it squeaks open, revealing a gloomy space with a dank smell. Throwing open the shutters of the small window, a lizard scampers away, startling me. The sunlight warms the tiny office, highlighting cobwebs in the corners. Looking around I speculate that the hospital cleaner seldom dusts this office, which is unfortunate, for it's in this space the midwives give results to pregnant women who've tested positive.

I retrieve the Kwejuna Project's register, buried under forms scattered on the desk. This legal-sized notebook contains all the relevant information on each woman: date of visit, name, age, due date, husband's name, village, local mayor, parish, sub-county, confirmation she received nevirapine, plus the initials of the person conducting the visit. From the beginning, Scott has copied all this data into an Excel file, a printout of which he's given me to use in the field. Updating this based on my outreach visits will now be one of my tasks.

Removing the paperwork from my backpack, I locate Zaituni's entry and then flip through the register, looking for her corresponding record. The visit summary confirms she should have delivered in early October, making her baby six weeks old. So, what happened? It's as if her child never existed. I scan Zaituni's information again and replay our conversation. She told us, plainly, she didn't have a baby. Her expression didn't change at all.

Could she have been grieving her dead child?

Grief, I conclude, has many faces.


Searching for women gets easier as I continue going out with Masika, and the motorcycle rides are far less intimidating than the first one. This morning, we're staying local, hoping to find women who live within walking distance of the mission.

'So, does he know who we're looking for?' I ask.

'Chairman knows one of the women. She's the second wife of a certain man. He told me she sells fish in the market.' Masika and I have just wrapped up a visit with the village head whose compound is several houses away from the duplex. Our path joins the main road. We follow it past the mango tree at the Christ School gate. At the fork, Masika steers me in the direction of her salon.

'Wait, I thought we were going to the market.'

'Yes, but I'm taking you behind, to the back. I go alone where they sell fish. I bring her to my place. If you go, people will talk.' She's right. As an outsider, I manage to attract unwanted attention, so there's no point in protesting.

When we reach Masika's salon, we find a young woman standing over a client, pulling a hot comb over her head. The place smells of burned hair. Masika takes out a stool for me. As I sit, she whispers, 'Let me come,' and ducks out. While observing the hairdresser cajoling her client's hair into submission with thick, strong fingers, I muse about all the chemically treated hair I've seen here. I didn't grow up around it – plaiting hair was much more common when I was young – and it's not something I expected in a place with such poverty. And yet it shouldn't surprise me because even when daily life is very, very hard, women here, like those the world over, desire to look beautiful.

Masika returns with Roseti, a baby-faced woman who can't be more than eighteen. She's petite and her hair is covered in a red scarf. Slipping in behind the gauze curtain, the two of them squeeze together on the remaining bench. We all exchange greetings but I hold off on my questions about her baby. In silence, we watch the hairdresser finish straightening the client's hair, only to curl it with rollers. When the client leaves fifteen minutes later, the hairdresser excuses herself too, and Masika closes one of the metal double doors to give us more privacy.

I thank Roseti for coming. Then with Masika translating, I explain our interest in following up on the baby she was pregnant with when she came to the clinic in June. Almost immediately, her expression changes. She begins to stammer. Her eyes fill and then overflow. Words come out one by one, as if with each syllable she's reliving the sorrow of her stillbirth at thirty-eight weeks. Though three months ago now, the pain is real and easily triggered. We pause, trying to create more safety for her grief to surface. We'd like more information but want to respect her sorrow and honour her sadness. She blinks and composes herself. We're so sorry, Masika tells her. Roseti looks down, concealing her face.

After several minutes, I press on. Does her husband know she was in Kwejuna? No. Would he be willing to come to the clinic for a test? No. Is she sure? Yes, he will refuse. That's as far as we can go. After allowing her tears to flow for some more difficult moments, we thank Roseti. She wipes her face with her scarf, ties it back onto her head, and disappears. Masika and I remain, still not making eye contact. Then, I pull out my clipboard. Another baby gone.

Evening has come and the duplex is calm. This is one of my favourite times of the day here. It's pitch black, which means few are moving around, and visits and requests for help at the door, of which there are many, have subsided. At this hour, people are settling down in front of outdoor fires, eating their main meal. During dinner with Pat, a persistent cricket chirps outside, hidden in the darkness, as I tell her about Roseti and ponder the number of Kwejuna women with dead babies.

'There's a lot of death here,' she says. 'It's something you never get used to.'

'I wonder how it impacts people in the long run?'

'Hard to say, but we have to believe God will redeem these deaths. He'll ultimately bring something good out of them.' My head tells me this is true; my heart right now says otherwise.

We clear the plates and move over to the living room with our wine glasses. Pat brings out some chocolate that friends have sent her from America and begins to tell me about Christmas in Bundibugyo.

'People are more relaxed. There's lots of visiting and partying because of the extra cash from cocoa. Christmas is also the one time of the year when everyone, no matter how poor, eats beef. And most people do whatever they can to buy new clothes too.'

'Do you get a lot of requests?'

'Oh yes,' she says, laughing. 'More than usual. Requests for money have already started coming, probably because people have heard I won't be here this year.'

'You'll be gone?' I turn to look at Pat but she's emptying her glass.

'I leave on the 15th, to be with my mom in Winston-Salem. She's ninety and having a hard time managing on her own. This may be her last Christmas in her home.'

I frown. Pat doesn't notice.

'It's so good of you to go,' I say, steadying my voice to suppress my shock.

'I really want to be with my mom,' Pat tells me, 'but I feel guilty about leaving, especially at Christmas.' I watch her without asking what she means. 'The Ugandans have seen so many of us come and go over the years, my friends are convinced that at some point when I go to the US, I won't come back. Of course, that's ridiculous.'

Fidgeting, I cross and uncross my legs.

Pat continues, 'Bethany's going home too, to Tennessee, but we'll both be back in January, for the retreat.'

My shoulders sag and a heaviness settles on them, but I don't express my disappointment. I should be OK with this. However, just when we are moving from being housemates to becoming friends, Pat will be leaving, a few days after Scott and his family. And if that weren't bad enough, Bethany's going with her. So, in mid-December, both of the women I live with will be gone. By then, Scott and Jennifer will have gone too.

Can anything else go awry while I'm here?

# 9
# The Phone Calls

My housemates will fly out in ten days. During their eighteen-hour stopover in London, Pat and Bethany plan to see *Les Misérables*. Bethany is even reading Victor Hugo's epic novel in preparation. On Saturdays, they've been scouring the second-hand clothing market at Nyahuka to find warm, trendy clothes suitable for London's West End. I envy their shared plans and feel like an intruder who has stepped onto the dance floor seconds before the last song of the evening is about to end.

Their impending departure, when I'll become the sole occupant in the duplex in this Ugandan village, has begun to affect my sleep. Often, I drop off when I first get into bed but awake in the wee hours and toss and turn, eager for daybreak to chase away the darkness. I dread nights like these when the minutes seem to slow down. They risk bringing the unexpected, like that time in Brooklyn, five years ago, when I was losing sleep, fretting over finding a new place to live.

\* \* \*

I had been in that neighbourhood for eight years, during which time I completed my PhD, and in that cosy studio apartment on my own for the last two. But I'd decided it was time to leave. Except for where I laid my head at night and the tennis courts at Fort Greene Park, where I spent weekend afternoons, the meaningful aspects of my life had moved out of Brooklyn. Every weekday I commuted via train and bus to the South

Bronx, seventy-five minutes each way. On Sundays, I was no longer attending a local church but was now going into Manhattan for worship. The long hours I spent on the subway were zapping my enthusiasm, and my energy.

My priority was a shorter commute. I had identified the perfect area in northern Manhattan: Hudson Heights, a tree-filled community bordering the southern edge of Fort Tryon Park. I could get a bus from there which would drop me two minutes' walk from the health department building where my office was.

But I'd been dreading the process of looking for a new place. Everybody knew that finding a decent apartment in New York was incredibly stressful – and expensive. As I lay awake that night fretting about when to start the process and juggling figures to try to stretch my budget, I heard my answering machine click. The previous week, I had received several strange phone calls from a drunk-sounding man whom I didn't know. I didn't think he knew where I lived, but he frightened me. My phone was cheap, had no volume control, and the ring was piercing, so at night, I had begun turning off my ringer along with the volume on my machine.

As I heard the tape turning, at the last minute I decided to listen to the message. Adjusting the volume, I recognised the voice. It was my younger sister phoning from Nigeria.

'… When you get this message, call the house immediately.' As she finished that sentence, her voice broke.

I grabbed the phone, but it was too late.

A hollow dial tone answered back.

* * *

Since that call from my sister, I've learned to tolerate stretches of sleeplessness better than I used to. No matter how long the wait, I know morning will come. As I lie there encased in the white mosquito net, out of the Ugandan night I hear a voice through my bedroom window.

'Pamela, this is Scott.' Though loud, he's calm. 'I need you to wake Pat up.'

The room is black so I can't see anyone, but my window faces the front. Scott must be on the other side of it. This is a strange demand at a bizarre hour, but because I'm not asleep, I respond with: 'OK.' Fumbling for the light I keep beside my bed, my fingers find it and switch it on. I get up, throw on a sweatshirt, and tiptoe next door to Pat's room. I call out her name, raising my voice a little each time. After the fourth time around, she stirs.

'Scott needs to talk to you. He's outside.' Her eyelids open, heavy with sleep. Perhaps she thinks she's dreaming. I am a new house guest after all, and this is odd.

'Scott needs to talk to you. I'm going to let him in.' I leave Pat and go to the door. When Scott follows me into the living room, Pat's standing there in her dressing gown. I turn to go into my room, but Scott tells me to stay and invites us to sit.

'Pat, it's your mom. She fell.'

'Oh no. Is she OK?'

'Her next-door neighbour found her. She's lost consciousness. Sounds like she's had a stroke. She's in the hospital. Your brother's been trying to reach you but couldn't get through.'

'I turned off my phone last night.'

'He couldn't get a hold of you, so he called me.'

Pat nods, her face expressionless.

'Your mom seems stable, but the prognosis is unclear. You should leave for the States as soon as you can. You were planning to leave next week, but you shouldn't wait. I'll call MAF as soon as they open, to get them to fly in tomorrow for you. Get in touch with the airlines. See what they can do to get you home quickly.'

Pat receives all of this news with no outward emotion. I embrace her, but she remains strong. No collapsing on me, no tears. She calmly locates her cell phone and goes outside to call her family. Standing in our backyard with Scott at her side, she speaks first to her brother and then to her mother. Inside I hear her loud and clear through the glassless, screened windows.

'Mom, I love you so much. I'm coming to see you as soon as I can. Mom, can't wait to see you again to spend Christmas with you.'

She carries on an extended conversation with her ailing mother, declares her love for her despite the huge distance, so much so that I become confused. Is her mother really at the other end of the line? Has she already recovered from the stroke? Afterwards, Pat tells me the phone was pressed up to her mother's ear by her brother, who was holding it in place at her bedside. She wasn't conscious but that didn't matter to Pat.

Later, I overhear Pat making calls to change her travel plans. I wish I could hang around, be with her as she absorbs this terrible news, but I have a steering committee meeting to attend. These meetings only happen a few times a year and involve all the medical and public health heavyweights in the district deliberating over decisions related to the HIV programme. They take place at the hospital in Bundibugyo Town and can last for hours, Scott tells me. I was already anxious about this gathering before the news of Pat's mother, because of all the new people I would have to meet. Now I'm dreading the whole thing.

After breakfast, Scott, Jennifer and I drive to the meeting. It doesn't get started until the district medical director arrives. A jovial man, with a protruding belly, he saunters in an hour late. He begins with a tense discussion of 'top-up' salaries. These are extra funds the grant pays to support the Ministry of Health staff who do the HIV prevention work. It's a sore point since these bonuses won't continue indefinitely. As the discussion heats up, Scott's phone rings. He hands it to Jennifer, who steps outside. She returns several minutes later, her face not giving anything away. She scribbles a note to me: *Pat's mother died. MAF plane confirmed for tomorrow.* It's as if a small guava has been dropped into my throat. I try to tune in for the rest of the meeting but my mind is back at the duplex.

News of the death of Pat's mother spreads quickly. When I return in the early afternoon, our home is packed with sympathisers. Death is a common occurrence here. The lack of

81

refrigeration and the inability to preserve the body mean corpses are buried within a day of taking their last breath. The hours leading up to and following a burial draw in the entire community. Any pre-existing plans are put on hold. Mourners gather at the home of the deceased and then congregate at the graveside until the body is laid to rest.

In Pat's case, although her mother died in the States and none of the Ugandans has ever met her, that doesn't matter. They grieve anyway. When night comes, most of the visitors return home, but two friends, one who washes my clothes, and the other, a pastor's wife, insist on spending the night. Since Pat has done this for so many, they reciprocate her kindness. Instead of sleeping in her own bed, Pat joins them in the greeting room, bringing out three six-inch foam mattresses and bed sheets to pad the floor.

I move through the next twenty-four hours as if I'm in a fog, struggling to support Pat as she organises her things to leave the following day, while interacting with endless numbers of well-meaning visitors. I also feel myself beginning to grieve her departure, and sleep little for the second night in a row. The next morning, John, Pat's houseworker, drives us to the airstrip. Bethany is leaving too. Together, they'll fly from Bundibugyo to Entebbe and on to Nairobi, where Bethany will head to London as planned. Pat will go straight to the States. I'm glad for Pat's sake that she'll have company on those first two flights, but my head is spinning. Knowing Pat has just lost her mother brings to the surface my previous loss.

As we wait for the plane, Pat sheds no tears. I can't help but think she must still be in shock, that the reality of her mother's passing hasn't touched her yet. On the other hand, I'm having no trouble feeling for her. As she hugs me goodbye, I can no longer hold back. Everyone else seems to be able to restrain their sadness, but I'm losing control. My eyes can't contain the deluge of tears forming there. The Ugandan children, who take great delight in staring at foreigners in ordinary circumstances, notice my damp, tear-stained face. Some of them smirk, not understanding why I'm so emotional in public here. Adults, both men and women, weep without shame when death occurs here, but usually in the presence of the corpse, and this one is far from Bundibugyo. My grief threatens to overwhelm me as I recall that missed phone call from my sister.

* * *

I was holding the handset, but she was gone. Her faltering voice had said it all, though. I told myself it must be Papa. I had last spoken to him two weeks before, on Father's Day. He had sounded upbeat and jovial and we'd had a good conversation. I wasn't aware that he was sick, but at my last visit at Christmas, he seemed frailer. A pinched nerve in his spinal column, a condition he'd endured for many years, was accelerating his ageing process. Perhaps now he'd fallen while bathing.

When I first left home for university in the US seventeen years ago, I had often feared I would receive a dreaded phone call in the middle of the night bearing awful news. But as the years slipped away and now that I had stopped thinking about such a call, that terrible situation had happened. I was sure of it. I dialled home remembering that since Nigeria is five hours ahead of Brooklyn, it was a little after nine there on a Tuesday morning. After several rings, a young man answered the phone.

'Hello, Brown-Peterside residence.'

Without even saying hello, I demanded to speak to my sister.

'She's not here.'

'What do you mean she's not there?' I began to raise my voice, the speed of my words quickening. 'This is Pamela from New York. She just phoned me.'

'She went to a call centre. She'll be back soon.'

In my confusion, I had forgotten we could no longer make international calls from the house. It had become too expensive.

'OK, let me hold until she comes back.' I hesitate, and then change my mind. 'No, please go and call Uncle.'

This young man, whose voice I didn't recognise, must be the receptionist at my father's office which is adjacent to my parent's home. During the day, the phone rings at both the house and the office so that if no one's at home, the office staff can take the call.

'Wait, is my father OK?'

'Let me go and call Uncle.'

Uncle is my father's younger brother who lives next door with his wife and daughter. He came to the phone after several minutes. I barely said hello to him either before I asked, 'Is Papa OK?'

'Your father is very, very, very, very sick,' he told me with a sombre tone that was unusual for him.

'What's wrong with him? Did he fall? Can he talk? Is he conscious?'

'No, he didn't fall.' Ignoring my other questions, he just kept repeating that Papa was very, very sick.

'How long has he been sick?'

'For a few days now.'

'I'm coming. I want to see him. Don't do anything to him before I come.' I didn't know what was going on, but Papa wasn't well. I wanted to be involved, somehow, despite being so far away.

He continued to listen while I ranted on and then told me my sister was back.

'She's just come in. Speak to her.'

Moments later, my sister took the call and mumbled a weak, 'Hello?'

'What's going on? Is Papa OK? What's happened?'

She hesitated for a moment and then said, 'Papa's dead,' beginning to sob. My knees buckled and I dropped to the bed.

'What?' I had known something was wrong, but I'd believed Uncle. 'Are you sure? What happened? When did he die?' She started to whisper between tears and I began to weep.

\* \* \*

I didn't see or hear from Pat once she left for Winston-Salem. I never even thought to email her, but I tried to remember to pray for her. Making funeral arrangements and hosting visitors fill the days following the death of a parent or any loved one. The profound loss you've experienced doesn't really begin to settle in until that flurry of activity has died down, when people have returned to the safety and rhythms of their own lives.

I couldn't help but feel sad that Pat didn't get to share one last Christmas with her mother, or that she hadn't been able to get to the US in time to see her alive again, even if it had been in a hospital room.

Of course, I didn't receive that opportunity either.

Less than forty-eight hours after I got my sister's call, I flew to Nigeria. It took us two weeks and two days to make all the plans to bury Papa. We even had to pick out a plot. Fortunately, we were able to persuade the vicar at St Piran's to squeeze him into their cemetery even though Papa hadn't attended any services there for a long time. St Piran's, named after the patron saint of tin since Jos was founded as a tin-mining town, was the Anglican church we attended as a family when I was growing up. In the final years of his life, Papa had had difficulty walking due to his progressive disability. Then he developed a weak bladder. That combination had discouraged him from attending lengthy outings like those church services.

On a crisp July morning, the same day that JFK Jr's plane fell out of the sky off the coast of Martha's Vineyard, we buried Papa in a simple but heavy wooden casket. The pall-bearers, all younger lawyers who had worked with him, leaned under its weight as they carried him from the sanctuary to the cemetery beside it. Papa was born in Jos, practised law in Jos, and died there too. There was a gracious symmetry in that. Though he'd travelled to countries flung across five continents in his sixty-seven years, he got one of his final wishes: to be buried wherever he died. As the casket was lowered into the opening in the ground with us all crowded around it, my aunt's seven-year-old grandson, whom Papa treated like the grandson he'd never had, pierced the air with a wail.

When I hear that haunting sound here in Bundibugyo, it signals another family is in mourning.

# 10
# The Training

Pat has been gone for two weeks and it's been hard, alone in the duplex. I'm tossing and turning a lot at night, vacillating between worry about the training Scott and I are planning and dread for when he leaves. On high alert, every time I hear a lizard scuttling in the rafters or birds' wings flapping between the ceiling and the roof, my shoulders tense up. When the occasional lorry rumbles by, to or from the Congo border, my mind conjures up all sorts of scenarios about the contraband that may be moving through the darkness in these desolate hours.

The afternoons are stressful too. Despite my very limited Lubwisi, when I return from my outings, people flock to my door. Kids come after school wanting a glass of cold water or biscuits or sweets or notebooks or pens, or anything else they can get me to give them. Adults do the same. If I'm feeling charitable, they may get a small gift, but these persistent requests are already tiresome. I've discovered how little compassion I have. Today, just before sundown, a man came asking for taxi money to take his son, who has sickle cell, to Bundibugyo Hospital. Desperate for the little boy to have a blood transfusion, the father, on the verge of tears, pleaded with me. I gave him USh5,000 (about £1.65). I wish I'd given more.

As I'm clearing the dinner table and deriding my lack of generosity, I hear, '*Kodi, kodi.*' Yet another knock at my door. I hesitate, reluctant to answer. Perhaps they'll go away if I pretend I don't hear them. *'Kodi, kodi.'* It comes again. This time I recognise the voice. It's Robinah, a sixteen-year-old friend of Pat's. I sigh. I don't have the energy for a visit tonight, but before I've decided whether I'll continue to ignore that knocking, Robinah has pushed back the curtain and waltzed into the living room. I must have left my door open after talking to that distressed father.

'Hello, Robinah,' I say, willing myself to be welcoming and offering half a smile.

'Pam.Ella, hello. How are you?' She's pronouncing my name the way Nigerians say it, something I find comforting, most of the time. As dark as charcoal, with olive-shaped eyes, thin lips and her hair pulled back into a bun, Robinah's profile reminds me of a soap ad I saw as a child, whose logo bore the silhouette of a beautiful African woman's face.

'I'm OK. You?' I notice she's carrying a black plastic bag. 'You brought your knitting?' The girls at Christ School are learning to knit and Robinah is an enthusiastic adopter. Since the term is over, she's living with her parents in Nyahuka. I met her when she visited Pat here a couple of times before she left. Unlike most of the other visitors I get, Robinah is comfortable having lengthy conversations in English. Still, I'm not sure how to navigate this potential friendship.

'I was hoping to use Pat's needle, the round one,' Robinah tells me, an inquisitive look on her face.

'Let me see if I can find it,' I say. This is not going to be a short visit.

Robinah plops herself down on the couch and begins to thumb through a magazine, the pages rustling, as I leave the room. I return with Pat's supplies and hand them to her.

'Ah, here it is,' she says after rummaging around in the bag and extracting a c-shaped needle. She takes out her knitting and settles in. I sit opposite Robinah, but with no knitting of my own, I watch her hands at work, frustration mounting.

'How is Pat?' she asks, oblivious.

'I haven't heard from her since she left,' I say, doing my best to tune in and engage. 'I'm sure she's busy planning the funeral.'

Robinah shrugs and continues teasing the wool between her needles. A few moments pass without either of us saying anything.

'Remind me, when will you be getting your results?' I ask.

Robinah shrugs again. 'It could be several months, maybe even next year before they release our O levels.'

'So, you'll be around for a while?'

'Seems so.'

'Will you be around next week?'

'I should be. Why?'

'The American ambassador's coming to visit Kwejuna.'

'The ambassador's coming here? From Kampala?'

'Yes, next Thursday. For the first time. Scott's decided to have a training with the TBAs while he's here. We're going to tell them about Kwejuna.' TBAs, traditional birth attendants, are lay midwives who deliver most of the babies in this district. 'They'll be here for two days, spending the night in the community centre. We'll hire someone to cook lunch but need people to serve it and wash the plates afterwards.'

'How many are you expecting?'

'A big group. About 250.' Robinah looks up at me.

'I won't be doing it alone, will I?'

'No, no. I'll ask some other girls from Christ School too.' Robinah keeps staring. 'Oh,' I say, 'and I'll give you something for helping.' She nods, her eyes dropping down to focus on her hands.

As the evening wears on, our conversation thins, filled with longer and more frequent silences. I try to stay relaxed but my chest begins to tighten. My frustration turns to irritation. I alternate between flipping through the magazine that's in the living room, one I've already read, and sitting there vexed. After more than an hour, with me now chewing on the inside of my cheek, Robinah decides to leave. When I walk her to the road, it's pitch black. Flying insects clamour to the beam of my torchlight and night creatures serenade us. I wave her off.

'Thanks Pam.Ella. See you on Thursday.'

'See you. Goodnight.'

Finding my way through the darkness back towards the glow of the duplex, I exhale, bringing some relief to the tension I feel. I envy how comfortable Robinah seems in Pat's home. Even more so than I am, it appears. I'm sad about my ambivalence towards her. Perhaps I just don't know Robinah well enough yet. Feeling ashamed about having these thoughts, I pull my door shut and lock it, thankful that she can help out next week.

The visitors at my door and trying to be a friend to Robinah are not the only things that are challenging. I'm also having a hard time warming to Alex. We've had a lukewarm relationship from the start, though I'm not sure why. We don't interact much since many of my days are spent looking for Kwejuna women, but whenever we see each other, usually at the health centre when I'm there to check on our nevirapine supply or gather data to update the Excel sheet, I don't find him friendly.

Scott's having issues with Alex too, trying to assess his commitment to the job. It doesn't help that Joseph, Alex's counterpart at the hospital, is a stellar employee: well-liked, hard-working, motivated and resourceful.

The day before the ambassador comes, things with Alex come to a head.

When I arrive at Scott's home for a meeting to finalise the training, which starts tomorrow, he looks shattered. Dark shadows encircle his eyes. Deep lines bury into his forehead.

Once we're seated, he tells me in a quiet voice, 'Yesterday a trusted friend saw Alex on a motorcycle with a large roll of plastic rubber sheets. I didn't want to believe it so I went into the Kwejuna office this morning to check.' He hesitates. 'I just bought four rolls. Now, there are only three in there. We couldn't have gone through a whole roll in two weeks.'

The roll is the width of a large rubbish bag but made of tougher plastic. Cut into sheets, these line the delivery tables during birth. Kwejuna provides these, along with a blade for cutting the umbilical cord, string for tying it, rubber gloves, and a new *kitenge* for the baby. Put together to form mama kits, these are essential supplies for the midwives which the government can't afford. They're also an incentive for women to have their babies at a health centre, rather than at home. Ironically, it was these very kits Alex was carrying on his bicycle when I first met him.

Scott buys supplies for the kits in bulk, in Kampala or Fort Portal. Once the materials arrive in the Kwejuna office, Alex spends much of his time cutting up the rolls, assembling the kits and keeping the health centre well supplied. With close to thirty births a month, this is a never-ending task, especially since all mothers in labour, regardless of their HIV status, are given one.

'Alex took plastic sheets?' I ask perplexed. 'Wonder why he took those?' The items in the kit don't seem of much value, except the *kitenges*. These pieces of coloured cloth – rich tapestries of reds, yellows, blues, oranges, greens and purples woven together with black and white threads in beautiful combinations – are for wrapping around each newborn. The free *kitenges* are encouraging more women to come to the health centres to have their babies, just as Scott and Jennifer hoped they would.

'It's really too bad,' Scott says, shaking his head. 'I'm not sure what to do but I need to talk to him about it. If he took them, and right now it doesn't look good, I'll have to let him go.'

'What would he be doing with a roll of sheets?' I'm still confused.

'Selling it, probably.' Scott takes off his glasses and rubs his eyes. 'I'll talk to him. Since we're already in December, I may just let his contract wind down at the end of the year.' After a moment, he says, 'Yes, if it turns out he took it, I won't renew his contract.'

The ambassador's small jet touches down on a sunny Thursday morning. In an effusive display of Ugandan hospitality, young people from a primary school welcome him with a boisterous performance. Preadolescent girls in white T-shirts pulled over their purple uniforms sing in unison. Straw skirts layer their waists as they sway to and fro, their near-shaved heads bobbing. Belting out songs containing the refrain, 'M-is-ta Am-bass-a-door, we are wel-com-ing you,' their a cappella voices ring clear and sweet. Male classmates harmonise along with them while beating two waist-high drums. The airstrip is packed with many nearby families, as well as staff from our funders, EGPAF, who drove from Kampala to participate.

After this warm reception, the entourage proceeds to Nyahuka Health Centre. When we arrive, another song-filled presentation awaits our guest. This time, TBAs, 248 women ranging in age from twenty-five to eighty, are the performers. Dressed in yellow Kwejuna Project T-shirts imprinted with the mother and children logo, they resemble an enormous collection of sunflowers swaying in the wind. To complete their uniform, they are each wearing a new pair of white wellington boots. The boots, stencilled with 'Kwejuna' on the side in bright red letters, are a source of great pride. Not only are they considered a status symbol because they're beyond the financial reach of most of these women, more importantly, they're protective. If worn whenever the TBAs are assisting a mother in labour, these boots will shield their feet and legs from being splattered with blood, some of which may be carrying HIV.

Holding up a newborn fashioned out of a thick roll of cloth, the TBAs dance and sing, celebrating the baby's birth, welcoming the ambassador in their unique way. A dark-haired, middle-aged man, he must be roasting in his navy blazer and tie given the thirty-degree sun. Still, he appears appreciative, a persistent smile on his face. I don't have a chance to meet him, but manage to snap several photos as the women surround him.

When the TBAs finish their performance, the ambassador goes off with Scott and Jennifer to tour Nyahuka. I amble back up the road with the lay midwives to the community centre. Because there are so many women talking and laughing among themselves, the one-kilometre walk takes longer than usual. I'm probably the only one who notices. Though I offer the occasional nod to feign interest whenever one of the women makes eye contact, I say little. My mind focused on the training, I pick at a hangnail on my thumb until it begins to bleed.

Though I have advanced degrees in public health, this sort of large group educational training is not my forte. I'm not a strong didactic teacher, nor do I relish the limelight. Nevertheless, I find myself standing in a large hall with windows that don't have glass, in front of a few hundred women crowded on benches, attempting to educate them in a language I can't speak, about how a virus we can't see can be passed from pregnant mothers to their babies.

Teaching using written words or sentences or having them read anything is out of the question since most of these women have a limited primary school education, so I use stories and stick figures whenever I can. After I speak, Masika repeats it in Lubwisi, followed by Alex who translates it into Lukonjo, the other language spoken here. I try to use simple sentences and talk slowly, but what I say ends up being translated into a series of short phrases. And then there's an ongoing double echo as it's repeated. This must be tiring for the women as well. Still, I do my best to cover the basics: what Kwejuna is, what HIV is, how it's transmitted, and how medicine can prevent transmission from mothers to babies . Finally, I encourage them to urge all pregnant women to get tested.

We wrap up with role plays. Robinah and the other girls who served the food help out, guiding what happens in small groups of women. I rotate around, eavesdropping and observing. There are many laughs and a few gaffs, but I'm encouraged watching the TBAs cheerfully applying what they've learned.

By one o'clock, my energy level is fading and a headache is threatening. Communicating verbally across a double language barrier to several hundred enthusiastic women for three hours has taken its toll. We assemble for a group photo before giving out a small gift to thank them.

When I announce that they will each receive USh10,000 (about £3.30), the hall echoes with applause. I blush with embarrassment at their gratitude. My eyes meet a TBA in the front row, who has a snow-white cropped afro and is probably the oldest woman there. She grins at me. I smile back, wondering how many babies she has helped enter this world. Then, when I explain they must sign for their money, I hear murmuring. The women turn to each other and start muttering. Joseph approaches me and whispers, 'They don't want to sign with a pen.'

'What do you mean?'

'They prefer to use their thumbs.'

'Their thumbs? How will they do that?'

'Don't worry. I brought an ink pad.' He grins and holds up a flat silver tin. So, just when I thought we were almost finished, it takes another hour for them to come up, one by one, and imprint their right thumbs onto the roster. By the time the last woman has left, the headache has taken hold and my temples are throbbing louder than the drums at the airstrip this morning.

Close to passing out from exhaustion or sleep deprivation or both, I pay Robinah and her friends, before grabbing my things, and dragging myself back to the duplex. When I let myself in, I shut my front door, unusual at 2.30 in the afternoon. As I do, I promise myself that no matter how loud or persistent the knocks, which are sure to come, I won't be able to respond to any of them before our team meeting in a couple of hours.

A short nap helps my fatigue, but as I'm walking over, a new apprehension sets in. My shoulders begin to feel heavy. During our last meeting with Scott and Jennifer before they leave, as we always do, we go around and share. Jennifer describes their time with the ambassador.

'We told him about the many responsibilities women face here. Not just the challenge of HIV, but the burdens they carry

93

as anchors for their families. As you can imagine, that led to a heated conversation with the staff.'

When it's my turn, I debrief the training and mention a follow-up one that I hope to do with the TBA leaders in January.

Scott has no problems with my idea. 'It's fine if you want to do that. We won't be back yet, but since it'll be just the leaders, should be much easier to manage.'

After pizza, there's no film. Scott and his family will drive out at dawn, and still have to finish packing. I'd like to wake up early to wave them off, as others offer to do, but know that isn't wise given my meltdown at the airstrip when Pat left. Our goodbye is brief.

'I'm sure you'll do a great job keeping Kwejuna going,' Scott says, embracing me.

'Thank you so much for being willing to stand in the gap for our family. It means more than you know,' Jennifer tells me. She hugs me too.

'I hope it's a really special time,' I murmur, stammering to get the words out. These are awkward moments, knowing they're leaving Uganda to care for her father during what could be his final Christmas. Feeling myself starting to choke up and not wanting to get tearful, I hurry away and step out into the dark night.

# 11
# The Letter

The email comes in the afternoon a week after Scott left. It's direct and clear: 'Attached is a termination letter for Alex. His contract will not be renewed. Don't review his case or get involved in a discussion with him. Plead ignorance, extend my condolences, and move on. I suggest you give the letter to Alex before he goes home to Kasese for the Christmas holidays.' I blink and look again at the screen. As I reread the note, a sick feeling comes over me.

Scott's request sounds reasonable. I'm now the acting director of Kwejuna and I knew Scott was considering this when we talked about Alex before he left. What Scott doesn't know is that the part about my job as project director in the Bronx that I disliked the most was doing this very thing: letting go of staff. I did this more times than I care to remember. Though I believe I always made the decision carefully and prayerfully, dismissing people had terrible consequences. When the end came, despite two write-ups and the final written warning, it seemed to be a surprise to the person being let go. And no matter how gently I tried to deliver the news, it was always painful.

Given the confidential nature of the process, the other staff hadn't been aware that for weeks, or even months, someone was in danger of being told to move on. When it happened, they were caught off guard. Losing a colleague often meant the end of a budding friendship, leaving those who remained hurt and angry. Any termination took long weeks for us to regroup after it and for me to regain the staff's trust and confidence.

The toughest instance was with Geraldine. We'd brought her in to fill a new position to help us boost enrolment in our studies. Geraldine was eager and ambitious. She won me over during the interview, and so I expected she'd be able to do the same for our prospective clients. But she had a shaky start and the learning curve was steep. When her initial six months were over, I extended her probation to give her more time to show that her efforts could make a difference. Despite her brave attempts and hard work, in the end, the evidence was in the numbers, or rather, lack of them. Still, it was a difficult decision.

When I let her go, the others were livid. 'She was our friend,' they cried. 'Why did you keep her around so long if you weren't planning for her to stay? We got used to having her here.' In giving Geraldine a fair chance to prove herself, it had backfired. I felt I couldn't win. When I said goodbye to the Bronx, I thought I'd left behind the responsibility of having to dismiss an employee again.

I was mistaken.

I sit up straight and take a slow, deep breath. Then, dismissing the anxiety that's lodged along my shoulders to the base of my neck, I open the attached letter to Alex. It is brief but cordial. Scott wants it delivered before the holidays. That's several weeks away, but with Alex already on a leave of absence which began when Scott left, he could take off at any time, without my knowing. Time is short. The team are going to Fort Portal, three hours from here and over the mountains, for a brief but much-needed pre-Christmas break. We head out tomorrow afternoon. It will be my first visit outside Bundibugyo and I've been counting on a relaxing weekend away. With a smouldering sense of dread, I realise I have to deliver this letter before we go.

As if he anticipates what's coming, Alex shows up at my front door the next morning before I've left the house. I greet him as usual, concealing my surprise. After he comes inside, he takes me further off guard, by asking, 'Do you have a letter for me from Dr Scott?' I didn't expect him to know about this. Scott must have phoned or texted him.

'Yes, Dr Scott sent a letter for you through the computer,' I say, doing my best not to change my facial expression or tone of voice. 'I haven't had time to print it, so I can't give it to you now.'

That's true but I'm stalling. I've asked Michael, who's now co-leading the team with Karen in Scott and Jennifer's absence, to be with me when I give Alex the letter. He's willing but isn't here right now. I feel awkward going outside to get a signal to call Michael because I don't want Alex to overhear the conversation. Besides, I wasn't prepared for this. I need to gear myself up to deliver this letter when I'm ready to do it, not when I feel Alex is forcing my hand.

'I have some other things to do this morning. If you come back by twelve, I'll have the letter ready.'

Alex agrees to return. At 12.50, there's no sign of him. Michael and I have been waiting for an hour. I skipped lunch because my appetite had disappeared. Now, I can taste bile in the back of my throat. We're meant to leave for Fort Portal in a couple of hours.

I phone Alex, the handset throbbing in my hand.

'Is the letter nice?' he asks me.

'You have to read it yourself and decide. Where are you?' I demand, irritation coating my words.

'I'm busy at the health centre. The nurses are on break.' This doesn't make any sense. Alex's role and those of the nurses don't overlap, but this is not the time to contradict him.

'I'm coming there now.'

We speed down to the health centre in Michael's beat-up pick-up. In the three minutes it takes us to get there, Alex has disappeared. Since it's the lunch hour, the only staff I encounter are in the lab. The two technicians reveal nothing. When I ask if they've seen Alex, they don't give a straight answer.

'But I just called him and he told me was here,' I rant. It does no good. I call him again.

'Alex, I'm at the health centre. Where are you?' I enquire, my voice pleading.

'I have to go to Bundibugyo Town. Now. Just keep the letter until you return.' Click.

I ring back right away but he's turned off his phone. 'The number you are calling is not available at the moment' is the last thing I want to hear. I hang up, my eyes filling with tears. Fighting to keep my emotions under control, I slide onto the front seat of the truck, trying not to cry.

'Michael, what should I do? This guy knows what's coming and thinks he can avoid it.'

Stroking his goatee, Michael suggests, 'We should find out where he lives and leave it there.'

'I have no idea where Alex lives,' I say, indignant.

'I'm sure Rogers will know. Aren't they good friends?' Michael asks. I say nothing. 'Let me see if I have his number.'

Michael scrolls through his phone.

'It's here. Should I call?'

'Please.'

Michael phones Rogers, a houseworker of Scott and Jennifer's, and gets directions to Alex's place. Minutes later we are squeezing through a narrow road behind the market where the afternoon heat has intensified the presence of an open sewer. People scatter. Heads turn. A lanky school-age boy looks up, makes eye contact with me and begins calling out, '*Muzungu, muzungu.*' I look away. We turn right and come upon a white building, like a storefront, with three dark-green doors. Two are ajar. One is shut with a bolt and heavy padlock.

'Alex's place is on the right.'

'Doesn't look like he's here.'

'We could leave the letter with someone.'

'No, I don't want to give him a reason to say he never got it. Let me try to slip it under his door.' I approach the third door, my heart racing, a small crowd of children that has gathered watching intently. As I do, a grey-haired man emerges from the middle doorway. I greet him and force a smile.

'*Olaayo Mzee, Alex, alliyo?*'

'*Talliyo ba.*'

'*Cale. Weebale.*'

Confirming that Alex is not around, I stoop to slide the envelope under the door. As I do, I feel the man's eyes and those of the children penetrating the back of my dress. With hands shaking, I push the letter in all the way. It takes a few tries before I'm sure that I've left not even a sliver of the white edge visible. Then, I stumble back to the truck.

'He can't claim he didn't get it,' I say, sounding more confident than I feel. Michael says nothing and we drive back in silence.

When Michael drops me off at the duplex, he reminds me, 'We'll be leaving at three. See you up at the house?'

I nod. 'Thanks, Michael, for everything.'

'It's what we do for each other around here.'

I drink some cold water and nibble at a cheese sandwich. Then I throw some clothes into an overnight bag and try without much success to unwind.

By 3.15, I'm back in Michael's truck on the way to Fort Portal for the first time. Squeezed into the front of the cab beside Karen, I'm grateful for the distraction of the kids in the back who're boisterous and excited about the trip. Right now, I want to get as far away from Bundibugyo as I can: the complicated friendships, the barrage of requests, the peering eyes, and now being responsible for letting someone know he's lost his job.

This long weekend has come just in time. I'm desperate for a break. The emotional toll of living here is wearing me down. This is all a lot more than I expected. If I can hang on through Christmas and into the new year, it's not too early to begin counting down the days until I leave.

# 12
# The Illness

The Monday after Christmas, news of a tsunami that obliterated Banda Aceh in Indonesia is all over the radio. I listen for a little while about waves crashing past beaches, swallowing up whole villages and racing into hotels, but instead of keeping me company, hearing about this terrible event heightens my sense of isolation. On my own in the duplex, and with the regular rhythm of going out to look for lost women on hold during the break, loneliness has crept in. Karen calls and invites me to go on a hike to the waterfall that supplies clean water to the area. I'm not keen, but since I'm less eager to spend the day by myself, I decide to go.

Besides the team, some Ugandan friends, including three Christ School girls, join us. The path is worn and the ridges to place your feet in are few. I do a lot of scrambling on my hands and knees, and where possible, grab tufts of grass to hoist myself up. As we get higher and higher hanging on to the outside of a mountain, when I make the mistake of looking down, the roofs far below begin to spin and the muscles in my throat tighten. I'm right at the back and try to concentrate on the girl ahead of me, who's overweight and wearing slippers, but she's struggling too.

'I can't do this,' she cries out at one point, tossing her footwear into a bag slung over her shoulder.

'Keep trying. We'll help you,' a young, muscular man up ahead calls out. She edges forward and I follow, but upon reaching a barren spot where the path is non-existent and there's nothing to hang on to, she crashes onto her bottom. As I come up behind her, I realise she hasn't fallen. She's plopped down.

'I want to go back. I'm afraid.' Her voice falters, as if she's on the verge of tears. The young man climbs down to grab her, letting others pass him, and pulls her up.

'You go ahead,' he offers. 'Let me come behind you.' Repositioning himself behind her, and in front of me, he cajoles her, and me. Step by step, tentatively, hesitantly, and with him continuing to encourage us at the back, we eventually reach the base of the waterfall. It's hidden inside the mountain, thundering down from two storeys above us. Up close, the runaway speed with which the water is racing brings on a new type of fright. I slide onto the ground right at its periphery, elated but cautious, my lungs wheezing. Then I see Karen and Michael's five-year-old daughter rush in. Facing the granite and shrouded in a sheet of water, she begins hopping up and down, her blonde head bobbing. Seeing her shake her body as if performing on a stage, and not wanting a child to show up my apprehension, I fling off my muddy shoes, peel off my soaked socks, and charge in too.

Returning home, my T-shirt and jeans drenched and clinging to me, my skin prickling with goosebumps, I'm ecstatic about accomplishing something I couldn't have achieved without the others, especially that Christ School girl. I reward myself by heating a kettle and taking a bucket bath with hot water. By evening, however, I begin to fall ill. Dryness at the back of my mouth has translated into a sore throat. I must be a little run down from the change of weather. With the rainy season over, the very hot, dry conditions that apparently come at the end of the year have arrived. The next day, I drag myself down to the health centre, reluctantly, to connect with the midwives and monitor the supply of mama kits and nevirapine.

I make it through the morning but by lunchtime I'm shattered. Perhaps I overdid it on the hike yesterday? Thigh and calf muscles I didn't know existed ache with every step. I go to bed earlier than usual that night, sleep in the next day, and skip the health centre. Good thing too, because Joseph stops by around 11.00 to pick up the letters for the TBAs. With Alex gone, he's taken on extra work.

'Oh, my goodness, Joseph, I completely forgot.' The letters are invitations for the leader training at the end of next week. 'Can we do this tomorrow?'

'Today is better. I'll do the women on this side of the district today and those on the Bundibugyo Town side tomorrow. For those in Rwebisengo and Ntoroko, I'll need more time.' I manage to type up and print the fourteen letters, but after Joseph leaves, I need to lie down. My strength is zapped. I stay inside for another day, listening to fallout from the tsunami. It's absolutely shocking. The numbers of dead climb into the hundreds of thousands.

The Thursday after Christmas, we gather at Michael and Karen's for a team meeting. I don't feel like myself but decide to go for the company. We spend much of our time planning how we'll see in the New Year, which begins in thirty-six hours. Afterwards we go around the room sharing what's on each of our minds. When I describe my symptoms, Anita, a Christ School teacher, suggests I take a malaria test.

'I don't think it's malaria, Anita. I've been taking a malaria tablet every Sunday.'

'Malaria pills don't necessarily prevent malaria. Just means if you get it, you'll get a milder form. Malaria's endemic here, so you should go ahead and take the test.'

'We have some tests here,' Karen offers, 'if you want to take one after the meeting.'

The finger stick test is negative and I'm disappointed. Yet, who in their right mind feels let down because they don't have malaria? I don't *want* to have malaria, I don't even want to be sick, but with malaria at least we know how to treat it: pump yourself with higher doses of malaria medicines, endure alternating cycles of chills and sweats, and wait for the fever to break.

On New Year's Eve, we gather at a large vacant house and each bring a dish which together make up a hearty meal of chilli, rice, corn bread and cabbage salad, but my appetite is flat and my throat's raw. I eat very little. After dinner, the party moves outside. We huddle around a bonfire. Despite its warmth, I shiver as my bottom gets damp from the dew on the grass. Leaning in closer to the dead wood cracking and hissing, the others laugh and tell stories. I don't join in. It hurts too much to talk. Besides, I'm exhausted.

Midnight arrives. The kids whoop and yell and chase each other around the yard. The others toast with glasses of wine, but I'm not drinking. My body is starting to ache and a sharp pain shoots through my throat whenever I swallow. When the fire smoulders and dies, we each settle into one of the many bedrooms. I find it hard to relax and don't sleep much. Early the next morning before anyone else is up, I dress and drag myself back to the duplex.

Over the next few hours, my condition gets worse. My throat is raging and I can taste blood. My body's getting weaker. What's happening to me? What will I do if this gets more severe? There are no doctors nearby. And, given that it's New Year's Day, I have no idea if there's a doctor on duty at the hospital. But even that is at least thirty minutes away on that perilous road and I wouldn't know if there was one there until I'd made the trip. Plus, I'd have to find someone to take me there.

My mind starts spinning out all sorts of worst-case scenarios. What if this becomes really serious and I can't get to a doctor? Am I going to end up dying alone in a strange house in a small village in the valley of the shadow of the Rwenzori Mountains? Could this be what God is asking of me? To risk my health and my very life to serve him here? Sweating, I fling damp bed sheets off myself.

By mid-afternoon, with my throat on fire and my body burning, I call Anita. Though not a nurse, in her resourceful way, she's taken on a quasi-nursing role for the girls at Christ School, handing out sanitary towels and pills – mostly antimalarials, antibiotics and ibuprofen – and doing malaria tests.

'Sounds like strep. I'll be right up and bring penicillin. Think you're going to need it.'

In fifteen minutes, she's at my front door toting a bag of pills.

'These are huge, like smarties and they're not even coated,' I protest.

'Let's see if you're going to need them.' Using a table knife to flatten my tongue, Anita peers down my constricted throat with the help of a small light she's brought.

'It's really red and swollen and there are some lumps on either side filled with pus.' I shudder. 'Yep, looks like strep,' she adds, confidently.

'Really?'

'Well, you can't be 100 per cent sure unless you do a culture, but I've seen strep many times. It looks the way your throat looks right now. Since a throat culture isn't really possible here without a lot of hassle, you should begin taking antibiotics. I'm pretty sure that's what you need.' She leaves me with forty monster pills, to take two, four times a day for the next five days.

I abhor taking pills. Memories of gagging often as a child come to mind as I recall the times when a stubborn pill would lodge itself in my narrow throat and I'd end up vomiting. Every Sunday evening in Nigeria, we took an antimalarial as well as cod liver oil. The oil looked like urine and tasted like petrol but slid down my throat with ease, so I was always more compliant taking the liquid medicine than contending with those malaria pills. Though smaller than an orange pip, they were white and uncoated and a nightmare for me to swallow.

I push these discouraging thoughts aside and focus instead on arranging the antibiotic pills into five clusters. Thinking a change of scenery might help me, I bring the blankets and pillow from my bed into the living room, along with some CDs and tapes and try to settle in for the night on the couch.

My throat burns and my sinuses are raging, but I know I have to take the first dose at least. I cut a pill in half. The smaller size seems more manageable, but also means I'll have to get this medicine down my ever-tightening throat more times. Ignoring that for now, I place the half-pill on the back of my tongue and take a huge gulp of water. My muscles protest. I gag and cough and spit out a soggy tablet into my hand, my tongue bitter and acrid. I wait a few minutes, try to regroup, and throw up a prayer. Then I try again, all the time forcing myself to remember that others who are far sicker than me – like those with AIDS – take more pills than I have to, not in the hopes of knocking out a single infection, but to counteract an insistent virus wreaking havoc on their immune system. And they'll have to do this every day for the rest of their lives. The pep talk and prayer help. I repeat that as the rest of the half-pills squeeze their way down, but not without considerable discomfort, a disgusting aftertaste and a lot of grimacing.

How will I keep this up for four more days?

During the night, I toss this way and that, trying not to swallow but acutely aware of the hurt slicing through my throat every time I do. Unable to sleep for long, I'm groggy and restless. When morning arrives, desperate to find an easier way to deal with the pills, I rummage around and discover several bottles of soft drinks in Pat's fridge. Soft drinks were my absolute favourite beverage as a teenager. Having reduced my sugar intake considerably since then, I avoid them, but in my current state I'm willing to drink almost anything to counteract the bitterness. I cut two pills in half, throw one half into the back of my mouth and gulp a huge mouthful of the syrupy liquid. It's far too sweet but the flavour soothes my mouth, coating the inflammation. The tablet edges down, drowned in a carbonated sea of sugar and chemicals. I down the remaining half-tablets the same way, finishing off most of the bottle.

Anita calls later that day.

'At least you're getting those pills down,' she laughs, hearing about me guzzling soft drinks. 'That's what counts. How're you feeling?'

'No change.'

'Give it a couple of days. I'm pretty sure the antibiotics will work.'

To pass the time while fighting strep, I scavenge around for something to read. My lack of sleep has left my eyelids heavy, my body limp. My attention span is limited too. I glance through several magazines. Then I flip through a book called *SONSHIP for Africa*. It was a gift from a couple I met at a conference just before I came here. After living and working in Kenya for many years, they had taken a US-based curriculum developed for pastors about how to live the Christian life as imperfect, broken people, and written a version for Africans.

When I got it, I'd been sceptical about whether non-Africans could create a convincing product for nationals that would be culturally meaningful and impactful. I still have my doubts, but on the page I open to, I begin reading an essay by the middle-aged pastor who has a doctoral degree. He describes his failures, and how for years, his motives for his work were, in his words, 'terribly flawed'.[1] He admits pursuing power and respectability in the name of success, which meant compromising his family and his vocation. His honesty is disarming so I keep reading.

I flip back a page and see a scripture passage there. A phrase from it catches my attention: 'in humility consider others better than yourselves' (Philippians 2:3).[2] I'm familiar with this verse but as I look again at those words, 'better than yourselves', I find myself wondering: how often do I do this? I think for a minute. And then I keep thinking. This is hard for me because I'd say I'm a pretty good person, but slowly I begin to feel convicted: if I'm really honest with myself, I do have a hard time thinking of certain people as better than me, especially those who seem less intelligent, less educated, less travelled, or even those with less money. As I admit these things to myself, a sense of shame, like a drop of food colouring staining a glass of water, spreads over me.

As I continue to contemplate this, my eyes fall on the words that come before those I've just read: 'Do nothing out of selfish ambition or vain conceit' (Philippians 2:3).[3] It's an imperative, as if someone is demanding it of me; I'd not noticed that before now. Then, as if bringing this statement into focus, the phrase 'selfish ambition' catches my attention. What exactly is 'selfish ambition'? I wonder. I'm not overly ambitious, am I? At least I don't consider myself ambitious in the typical, overt go-after-what-you-want, however-you-want it, type of way. Having lived in New York for the past fourteen years, there have always been people around me who were much more driven than I've been, even downright ruthless, in pursuing their goals and dreams. Besides, ambition, in and of itself, isn't necessarily a bad thing, is it?

What about ambition that's selfish? I try to swallow and then remember the pain I'm in, but can't seem to let go of these two words. Being selfish is not attractive, but what does 'selfish ambition' look like? Not sure. I think back to the pastor's self-described flaws and realise, like him, my ambitions have revolved around me and how my achievements would benefit me. I've pursued 'noble' goals, like public health and women's empowerment and AIDS prevention, but at their core, the reasons behind these pursuits haven't been primarily about others or for a greater good. I'm ashamed to admit it even to myself, but if I'm honest, they've served to fulfil my need to *be* somebody of significance, someone who's seen to be doing meaningful work. Along the way, I've sacrificed investing in friendships and relationships, even in having a family of my own.

This introspection is getting a bit too heavy for me.

I take myself to the bathing room and wash my face. Avoiding the mirror, I pat my face dry, but thoughts continue to flow. Settling back on the couch, I find myself reflecting on the career I've chosen. In academic public health, there are two clear markers of success: publications, which support research grants, and research grants, which lead to more publications. With a substantial enough record in both, you can usually look forward to being granted tenure and then becoming a professor.

I've published a few papers in respected public health journals and am proud of these. I've secured several modest grants to investigate the links between sexual risk among women and a history of trauma, accomplishments that have also brought a degree of satisfaction. Then, this past spring, I applied for a prestigious National Institutes of Health grant. After breaking all my own rules by working late into the night and on multiple weekends in an effort to submit what I thought was a stellar proposal, those reviewing the grant decided not to fund it. I was crushed, experiencing that rejection as a reliable measure of me as a researcher. In spite of my deep disappointment, or perhaps because of it, I hadn't been able to motivate myself to revise and resubmit the grant.

In the months following, as I'd wrestled with the decision to leave my job, I had wondered if perhaps I just hadn't wanted that grant badly enough. Perhaps I had too little ambition? Maybe, at this stage of my career, it's largely about persistence, and trying and trying again until you're successful. Maybe I wasn't tenacious enough or, could it be deeper than that, that I was no longer in the right job? Perhaps I was even in the wrong profession!

Failure to obtain that grant had forced me to admit that I was no longer able to keep up with my own exacting standards. This experience had also revealed how much my accomplishments were a measure of my sense of self. I'd become smug about the things I'd achieved. I didn't go around bragging, but derived great pride and a deep sense of worth from them. They helped me to feel better than others who were less accomplished.

When it came right down to it, I saw that the setback with the grant had exposed something far more entrenched and frightening. It had revealed that my approach to life, which had prioritised work and professional accomplishments as its central and defining aspect, was deeply flawed. Despite pursuing honourable endeavours, I had made vocational success more sacred than valuing people. I may not have chosen a cut-throat path or a lucrative one but, until I was flat on my back in a strange house in a village in Uganda, vulnerable and frightened, far from people I knew well, forcing myself to swallow large, horrible penicillin tablets, I came to see I had in fact spent years pursuing my 'selfish ambitions'.

No wonder exhaustion had chased me out of the Bronx.

As I stared at this simple phrase again, 'Do nothing out of selfish ambition or vain conceit' (Philippians 2:3),[4] I began to see that for most of my adult life, for the past twenty years, I'd lived in opposition to this. Personal ambition, with a generous dose of 'vain conceit', had controlled me. My face flushed with perspiration. My chest caved in. An acerbic taste that I couldn't blame on the antibiotics spread along my tongue. Until I let go of my job in New York City, deeply held desires to define myself by success had begun to crush me.

Had I failed them?

Or had they in fact failed me?


Anita's diagnosis of strep turns out to be right. I continue the pill ritual for the next seventy-two hours. Working my way through the two remaining soft drinks, I try not to dwell on the fact that I once heard, if you leave a tooth in a glass of one of these, in a week it will have dissolved. After three days of downing half-pills, I begin to feel less discomfort when I swallow. I'm able to drink other liquids and eat soft foods. By day four, I manage to prepare and eat French onion soup. On the fifth day, I can swallow without noticing it, a sure sign that the infection is gone. I down the two final half-pills with the last bottle in the fridge, triumphant that I've survived my first bout of strep throat, in rural Uganda, and without the care of a doctor.

# 13
## The Fallout

Joseph has delivered all the invitations for the leader training. However, the day before the women are to come, I have to concede I'm being unrealistic. The throat infection is gone but I haven't had the energy to map out the content for the event. I ring him that morning.

'Joseph, we're going to have to cancel the training tomorrow.' My breathing is laboured. 'I'm feeling better but my voice, it's not strong. Can you let the women know?' I'm still weak and just getting this out leaves me winded.

'I can reach those on this side of the district but for those on the Fort Portal side, it's too far for me to go there today to inform them.'

'Oh, Joseph, I feel terrible about this. What shall we do?'

'Make it for another day. I can meet the women at the community centre, tell them you are sick and give them a new date. But we should give them something for transport.'

'You don't think they'll be angry?'

'They will understand. What about doing it next week?'

'Let's make it Thursday. I should be well by then. Tomorrow, come early. I'll give you their transport money. Oh, and please tell Masika.'

I'm mortified to have to cancel the training. For some, it means walking a distance that will take more than two hours – only to have to turn around and go home again. All of them will come expecting a workshop, a decent meal and a cash gift at the end of it all. I hate being the source of their disappointment. The next morning, fretting that I'm letting them down, after I see Joseph, I keep my front door locked until midday, long after I know they will have come and gone.

'They were sad you are sick,' Joseph reports, handing me the record of the monies he gave out, 'but happy for the transport. They will come next week.' Only when he leaves do I allow myself to relax, relieved they were so gracious to me.

Several days later, as I begin to prepare, I realise it wasn't necessary for me to do this particular training at all. Because I felt unsure teaching such a large group in December and wasn't convinced all the women had learned how they could help with Kwejuna, I thought I should do more. Scott was supportive but since he would be gone, it was my decision. I was confident I could manage this smaller group on my own, but now that all the teaching and planning are up to me, I realise what a major undertaking it is.

I want to end well. Right after the training, we'll be making our way to the retreat in eastern Uganda, where those who've been in the States will join us. It will be my final week in the country. I'm ready for my time in Bundibugyo to be over, but before leaving, I feel compelled to make a lasting and positive impression. However, I have yet to learn how to ask for help. I know Karen and Anita won't be able to help with the teaching, but I don't think to ask them to organise the food – until it's all over. Instead I plough ahead on my own, working out a day's worth of relevant material, finding a friend of the mission to cook for us, and lining up Robinah and two other girls to serve lunch. All of this means I'm worn out before the training even begins.

The following Thursday, when I enter the community centre, the TBAs clap their hands together and cheer. All fourteen women have returned. The smile which spreads across my face can't express sufficiently my deep appreciation.

'*Weebale kwesa*, thank you for coming,' I repeat, over and over again until the clapping stops.

Since these women are leaders and all have some secondary schooling, I've decided to focus on helping them learn how to interpret the coded HIV test result used across Uganda, written on women's pink prenatal cards: TR means the patient is not infected; TRR indicates infection.

Though this seems like a simple difference, distinguishing these codes turns out to be too complicated for some women. They glow when they're able to locate the result on the card, since it isn't always written in the same place, but two of them are unable to differentiate between TR and TRR. One TBA, elegant in a pink dress, repeatedly points to the TR and declares with confidence that the woman is living with HIV. Tempted to shake my head, I conceal my dismay. Concluding a woman is living with HIV when she isn't will be a disaster, risking rumours, a ruined reputation and perhaps even abandonment.

I'm relieved when lunch arrives. It comes in pots steaming with rice and brimming with beans and beef and cabbage hauled up the road from Nyahuka in a wheelbarrow. We sit outside on the grass, dry from the lack of rain, in the shade of the building's shadow. When we finish eating, I leave Robinah and her friends to wash the plates while I try to undo the damage done in the morning. It's too late to change course, so I decide to keep the message very basic. Rather than fuss with interpreting codes, every TBA should be aware that there's medicine which can save the babies of positive mothers. They should encourage all pregnant women to come for prenatal care and HIV testing. I reinforce this through didactic teaching, role plays and simple quizzes, hoping by the end of the afternoon that message has stuck.

By the time we wrap up, despite teaching a much smaller group of women, on the heels of recovering from strep I'm shattered and my throat is parched. Weary, I'm convinced once and for all that I'm not cut out to be a trainer. After we reimburse the women for coming, they thank us and scatter.

Masika, Joseph and the girls who helped head out too, but Robinah lingers as I gather my things.

'Robinah, are you still here? You didn't need to wait for me, you know.'

'I know,' she says. 'Here, let me carry your basket.' She eases my training materials off my shoulder and slides them onto hers. We walk together to the duplex in silence. I can't wait to get inside, eager for time alone to decompress. When we reach my front door, I take the basket from her.

'Thank you for helping out today.' I step inside and go to pull the door shut when she calls out, 'Where's my gift?'

'Your gift?' I ask confused, looking right at her.

'Yes, my gift, for today,' her dark eyes flashing.

'Gift?' I ask again, puzzled.

'Aren't you going to give me anything for helping?'

'N-o. I never said I was going to give you anything. I asked you to help, but I didn't say I was going to pay you. This is different than the other training. There were twenty of us who ate today including the three of you. How can you compare that to serving lunch to that huge group of women who were here for the ambassador?' As I speak, I feel warmth seeping into my cheeks.

'I still think you should give us something,' she insists.

'I'm not going to. I'm sorry.'

Shaking her head and pursing her lips, Robinah sulks off towards the road. I close my door, my hands unsteady. Should I have paid Robinah and her friends? Am I being stingy? Perhaps. After all, I have so much more than she and her schoolmates. That admission brings a sense of shame. But even worse, now I feel embarrassed that Robinah has exposed my frugality. For half a second, I wonder if I should reconsider reimbursing them for their help after all. But I reason to myself, Robinah's on her way home, and the others left ages ago and they didn't even bring it up.

I decide to let it go, and two days later I leave Bundibugyo.

# 14
## The Exit

As we drive out of the district, the majestic Rwenzoris no longer fool me. I've lived beneath their watchful gaze. I now know something of the harshness that lies in the shadow of their valleys and I've witnessed up close the struggle for daily survival that they loom over. As we lurch back and forth over the switchbacks of the mountains, I recall the past tumultuous eleven weeks: the sense of abandonment I've felt, the pervasive presence of death, wrestling with illness, and seeing for the first time the ugliness of my own ambitious heart. Somehow, through all of this, God has sustained me and I'm so grateful, but would I ever want to come back here? I can't honestly say that I would.

After a night in Kampala, we make our way to a simple resort outside Jinja, a town close to the source of the Nile. The morning after we arrive, I rise before dawn. Wrapping myself in a red jumper, I pad down through the gardens to the edge of the water. Dew drenches the grass around my shoes and the bench where I sit, and unwelcome goosebumps spread all over my body. Trying to chase the cold away, I pull on my sleeves to stretch them beyond my fingertips.

The smell of raw fish drifts over the dark expanse of Lake Victoria. As a hint of the new day beckons, I make out the silhouettes of fishermen coming from a nearby village. Two of them bend over and scoop water out of their canoe. Replacing the water with a large net, they slip into their boat and paddle away from the lake's perimeter. More villagers appear in the shadows, talking in low voices. Like the others before them, the men empty their canoes and two by two, as if waltzing to a symphony only they can hear, they glide away in search of the morning's catch. When they disappear, women emerge, their bosoms and bottoms shaping their outlines, chatting with one another, swinging empty jerrycans. At the edge of the lake, they crouch to fill their large jugs. Then, hoisting them up and balancing them on their heads, their neck muscles taut with concentration, they haul water back to their homes.

As I continue to marvel at this scene, the sun's halo, a fiery ball, edges above the horizon. Yellows and pinks mingle with the mist lingering over the translucent lake. Though the beauty astounds me, at the same time, I'm struck by how helpless I am to stop this vista from unfolding. The sun will keep rising higher and higher, healing the darkness, transforming all that is before me into different colours, like a kaleidoscope. Before long, the magnificence of the early morning will have vanished, only to reappear with the next revolution of the earth. Change too is similar: sometimes jolting but more often gradual, imperceptible even, but always inevitable. As our surroundings shift, we're altered right along with them, in ways we're often not even aware of. The difference is, we don't revert back to who we were before the changes began. We've metamorphised into someone else.

Pat and Bethany, as well as Scott and Jennifer and their children, have returned from the US. They rejoin the rest of us here, along with several senior staff members from the mission, including the executive director, whom I've only met once before briefly in Philadelphia. Pat has been away for six long weeks. She knows nothing of what I've experienced living in her house by myself, as we've not spoken or emailed while she was away. Too absorbed in my own difficulties, I didn't contact her during her time of grief.

As I speculate about what it was like for her to return home to bury her mother, I wonder how her loss has impacted her. I know too well the suddenness of losing a parent. When it happened to me, I was afraid the grief would overwhelm me. At times, I wondered if my feet would ever find a firm place to stand. It took me about eighteen months to feel myself again after Papa died, even though his absence always remains. The truth is, God does meet you in your sorrow. He's there right with you all the time, and He does help you to claw back onto solid ground.

I want to share this with Pat and reassure her that she'll be OK, eventually. Even if she doesn't feel this way now. Even if she can't envision that for herself at this stage. I can still recall the terrifying weeks and months I lived through following Papa's death. For a year after his passing, I couldn't focus on a paragraph in a newspaper long enough to get through a whole story. To lose something that had been so enjoyable, that Papa himself introduced me to at a young age, was frightening and bewildering.

Then, two years later, when I had learned how to read again, for a number of months following the tragedy of 11th September, 'The City' section of *The New York Times* contained brief biographies of people who'd perished in the World Trade Center. Every Saturday morning as I read those stories at my kitchen table, tears would fall, enough to dampen the pages. I wept as if those profiled were my friends, though I had no personal connection to any of them. This wellspring of emotion caused me to revisit my own loss all over again.

I don't know how Pat's grief will manifest itself, or the ways it'll unsettle her, but I'm concerned. Though she's had her hair cut and it gives her face a more youthful look, I see the sadness lodged in her eyes and anguish burrowing in the lines around her jaw. After our initial long hug, on our second evening she tells me about the funeral and how some dear friends had attended.

'They drove all the way from Philadelphia to be there with me. I was so glad they came. It was a really hard time.' Her voice is steady, with no hint of emotion.

I remain quiet.

'They were so wonderful,' she continues, 'but you know, after the funeral, when everyone left, it was really hard going back to Mom's house.' Her eyes well up. A single tear spills out onto her cheek. She ignores it. 'Mom and I were going to spend Christmas together. It felt so empty and strange not having her there.'

'Being in her home must've been such a painful reminder that she was gone.'

'It was, but, you know,' she says, wiping her eyes and sniffling into a tissue, 'even though it's only been twenty-four hours, being back in Uganda has been so good for me. This is where my life is. This feels normal. And even though we're not in Bundibugyo, being here is familiar and I love being with the team. They're closer to me now than my own family.'

I stop her and put my left hand on her arm. 'Pat, that's great to hear, but how are you doing, you know, really doing?'

She hesitates and looks me in the eye. 'It's been really, really hard, but I'm OK. I really am doing OK. Despite all that's happened, I know God is still good.'

I look back at her. Her calm words amaze me. She seems so unflappable. Does she really mean this, or is she just more accustomed to grief than I was? I search her face again.

'I really am doing OK,' she repeats.

I say nothing, but turn away and mumble a silent prayer, begging for her kind of faith.

At breakfast the following morning, Scott and I sit together. After catching up and finding out that they've had a memorable Christmas with Jennifer's dad, Scott says he has something to tell me. I ease my chair back a bit and sit up.

'I've been doing some thinking.'

'Oh, about what?'

'About Kwejuna,' he says, looking at me, his eyes meeting mine. 'And its future.'

'What do you mean?' I ask, suddenly unsure about where this conversation might be going. Like that one in his Land Rover in my first week, I have a sense of déjà vu. Could they be leaving again?

'Well,' he says, waiting for a moment before going on. 'Jennifer and I think we should submit a renewal grant to EGPAF after all.'

'Interesting,' I say, not sure why he thinks this would be relevant for me.

'I've been in touch with their Kampala office,' Scott continues. 'They're very supportive. I know we'd get the money.'

'That's encouraging,' I add, still puzzled.

'More and more women are getting tested and coming to have their babies at the health centres. We could expand the programme to the whole district, to all seven health centres.'

'Makes sense.'

He looks down at the eggs on his plate before making eye contact again.

'I'd like you to come back and help us do that.'

My stomach heaves.

He goes on, 'I can't manage Kwejuna on my own. So... I don't think I'll apply for the money, unless you come back.' His eyes brighten. 'Instead of being the acting director, you'd be the assistant director.'

The muscles at the base of my neck tense up in protest. I focus on keeping the conversation practical.

'How long would the renewal be for?'

'Two years.'

Two years! I've barely survived three months in Bundibugyo. How would I cope for two years? I don't have the nerve to say this, so I try to buy myself some time.

'When would it start?'

'Well, I'd like to submit mid-year. The grant would start next January. We'd need you back here by then, ideally.' Tension moves down to my back. I keep myself talking.

'Scott, this is a lot to think about. When do I need to decide?'

'We don't want to rush you, but we'd like you to think it over in the coming weeks.'

Later that afternoon when the day's programme is over, I sit down outside at a small round table. A straw umbrella, woven like a basket, shades its surface. Journal and pen in hand, I stare out across the lake once again. I can hear cicadas chirping and, when the wind blows in my direction, I smell fresh fish. The village men and women I've seen the last two mornings are long gone. The sun inches westward, dominating the sky.

I've come here for some time alone to think through Scott's proposal. Do I really want to work with the Kwejuna Project long-term? Should I return to Bundibugyo for two more years? Is it a wise move? For my career? For me personally? This possibility mystifies me, terrifies me even. But I'm not able to dismiss the idea, either. I've wanted to work in Africa for a long time, so I need to give this proposition serious consideration. I look out at the body of water before me, marvelling that not far from here, it connects to Africa's longest river. At this hour, the lake is still and gleaming.

I try to focus. This decision is not as simple as whether to come back to Uganda or not. That would be hard enough, but I'd have to join the mission and become a bona fide missionary. That means I'd have to raise the funds needed to live here for two years. And all of this would have to happen within the next twelve months.

What should I do? What does God want me to do?

I want to do the right thing, but don't know what that is. To prevent emotional paralysis, I know I have to face my fears head-on. So, I decide to make a list of all that scares me about returning. Opening my journal, I peel my eyes away from the tranquillity of the water and begin scribbling:

1. Afraid of being unable to do this job. If I'm given greater responsibility, I could fail.
2. Afraid that I don't have the extroverted personality to keep up with Scott and Jennifer.
3. Afraid of being a disappointment, to them, to the Ugandans.
4. Afraid that if I do decide to come back, I won't be able to raise enough funds.
5. Afraid of the friends I'll lose if I'm gone from New York for such a long time –

'Mind if I join you?'

I take my time before looking up. When I do, towering above me is the mission's executive director, built like a bear with greying hair and a full beard. Without waiting for me to answer, he pulls up a chair. I feel a hint of anxiety slide into my throat. I hardly know this man. I've only met him once, when I went to the head office outside Philadelphia before I left the US to come to Uganda.

'It's really beautiful here, isn't it?' he says, extending his legs under the table as his eyes look out over the garden and the lake beyond it.

'I never realised Uganda would be so stunning,' I say, trying to sound relaxed. 'I thought Bundibugyo was incredible, but it's even more spectacular here.' At once, I regret mentioning Bundibugyo. Too late. He turns to look at me.

'So, what do you think? Will you come back to Bundibugyo? We'd love to have you.'

'Not sure. It's not an easy place. Was just making a list of all that scares me about the idea.' I wait for a few moments and then ask him, 'What do you think I should do?'

His gaze back on the water, he measures his response before saying, 'It depends.'

'On what?'

'Depends on what your priorities are. You need to think through those. It's very remote. You'd have to consider if you feel called to spend two years there, instead of being in New York, or somewhere else, where you'd have a whole different set of options.'

'That's true, but I think it's ultimately about calling. How do I know if this is what I'm called to?'

'Ah, that's between you and God. It'll take time before that becomes clear.' We sit together in silence, taking in the view. He continues, 'As I said, we'd love to have you, but take your time. Don't make a decision now. In fact, it would be better for you not to decide anything until you leave Uganda. Give yourself some distance. Gain some perspective. That can't happen while you're here.' Still looking out at the water, he adds, 'Then decide.' He slides back his chair and stands, flashing me a mischievous smile. 'You know how to reach us.'

I decide to take his advice. I ask Pat, Scott and Jennifer not to talk to me about whether I'll come back. I don't know how to consider the future, so I live fully in the present. In the early mornings I spend time down by the lake, during the day I sit in on meetings with the team and in the late afternoons I swim in the resort's pools, or read. In the evenings, I feast on whole grilled tilapia.

Relaxed and carefree, after breakfast on our final day, I decide to drop a note to Robinah. The time away from the district has already given me a clearer perspective. I recognise my part in the miscommunication we had. It wasn't unreasonable for Robinah to expect that I would give her and her friends some money for helping with the second training as I had done for the first one. There was no reason for me not to thank them in that way. I buy a card made out of banana fibre in the gift shop and write an apology. I don't know how Robinah will receive it, but if I return to Bundibugyo, it would be awkward to go back with that damaged friendship hanging in the mix. I write a few lines, seal the envelope, and give it to Pat to deliver.

With that, I leave Uganda, my conscience clear.

I fly across the continent and spend a few weeks in Jos. While there at church, I run into an old friend, an American, who'd been my younger sister's classmate. After university in the US, he'd married and returned to Jos to serve as a physical education teacher and coach at the international school we'd all attended.

'How've you been, Pamela? You're based in New York, right?' He had a lanky frame and, apart from contact lenses which had replaced his plastic-framed glasses, he'd changed little since I'd been gone.

'Yes, I'm in New York and you're still here,' I say, teasing him. He laughs. 'But I just spent three months in Uganda doing HIV prevention. With a mission organisation, can you believe it?'

'How was it?'

'Beautiful. I was in a village near the Congo border. Lots of poverty. Parts of it were hard, really hard, but they'd like me to come back for two years.' I hesitate. 'Not sure if I should.'

'What were you doing before that?'

'I was in the Bronx, doing similar HIV work with women. That was hard too,' I say, grinning. 'I seem to be drawn to hard places.'

He stares at me and then gently says, 'I'm sure there are quite a few people who could do what you were doing in the Bronx, but how many people could survive working in a Ugandan village? Takes someone unique. Maybe someone like you.' His words are convicting. I continue to return to them when I get back to New York in March.

Since I don't have a job here any more and am not sure about my future, I don't look for permanent work. I decide to temp as I continue thinking and praying about what to do. It's tough-going financially and I'm barely eking out a living. The agency places me with a progressive environmental non-profit organisation in mid-town Manhattan. I spend mornings opening envelopes containing cheques, large and small, and documenting the funds that have come in. The work doesn't stretch me and counting money in a season when I have little of my own isn't exactly a joy. In the afternoons, I try to look busy.

During my lunch hours, I sit in a nearby park, inhaling the fragrance of cherry blossom trees bursting into flower and basking in the possibilities inherent in spring, while I eat my home-made cheese sandwich and nibble on an apple. I'm still unsure about my future, but when the non-profit offers me a full-time job, I'm certain I want to do more with my life than tally other people's funds. One afternoon, heading back to the office, I walk past a large department store. The cheerful display of pastel blue, yellow and pink sandals advertising two pairs of flip-flops for the price of one charms me. Yet, on my penny-pinching budget, I can't even afford these cheap shoes. As I stand there and see my reflection in that window, I realise I really do want to live in Uganda again, where I can wear flip-flops every day if I choose to.

So, I repeat what I'd done fourteen months before, thinking this time around I'm more aware of what I'm signing up for, and more committed. I join the mission, take on some short-term consulting projects while I raise the necessary funds, find new tenants for my apartment and head back to Bundibugyo. Though it seems like a purely personal decision, I believe it's God who's called me back, for many reasons, some of which are apparent to me and others that will unfold over the next two years.

Arriving in Bundibugyo for the first time; Scott (r)

Children at the airstrip

Me and a friend

I lift my eyes to the hills

By the river

Traditional birth attendants celebrating

Ngite waterfall – source of safe drinking water

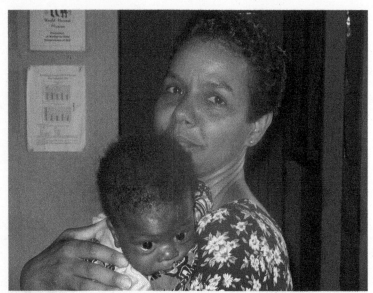

In the clinic

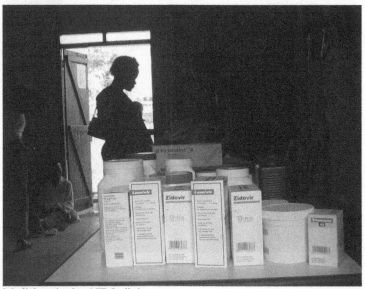

Medicines in the AIDS clinic

At the duplex

Pat and me

Jennifer and Jonah at the opening of the new paediatric and maternity building

Traditional birth attendants in their blue aprons

# Part Two

Part Two

# 15
## The Re-entry

The Wednesday HIV care clinic at Nyahuka is a mess. When registration begins, patients mob the front desk. Unable to wait for me or Masika, who's my translator again, to call out their name, they shove and grab, convinced they can spot their chart while reading upside down. There are at least sixty of these distinctive blue folders, each the size of an A2 sheet, and the number is growing. Locating the right chart for a patient can take fifteen minutes with no system to track them and no filing cabinet or drawer to house them. When a patient dies, and we've already had a few since I've begun coming here, the deceased's chart floats in among the others before one of us thinks to extract it from the pile of active cases. Sometimes a misplaced chart never surfaces in the three or more hours patients wait for their five minutes with the clinical officer and their two-week supply of medicine.

This inefficiency exasperates me.

Several weeks after entering into this mayhem, where my primary role in the clinic is to provide support wherever it's needed, my tolerance wears thin. I decide to set up a simple filing system. I start by purchasing six large rectangular plastic baskets, three for Bundibugyo Hospital and three for Nyahuka, where the two HIV care clinics take place. Yesterday I spent two hours organising the Nyahuka charts by surname and separating them into different baskets for women, children and men. I'll do the same at the hospital when I'm there on Friday.

At 9.45, I hop on my bike and head down to the clinic, chuffed with my efforts and hopeful for less chaos. The road is hard and cracked now that it's the middle of the dry season, and the shrubs and banana trees, usually lush, appear limp and in need of rain. The sky is cloudless, the sun baking. Five minutes later, and stepping in through the wooden double doors as I wipe the perspiration off my face, I take in the scene before me. Like other Wednesday mornings, the waiting area is already packed with about thirty people crammed beside each other on rows of benches. The atmosphere is buzzing with a cacophony of conversations. I detect a whiff of sugar melting into cornmeal and notice, in one corner, a group crowding around a young woman balancing a large tray of mugs on her right shoulder. Hands are reaching up and grabbing cups of thick porridge. Pat came up with this idea of providing a substantial snack for the patients to eat to make these lengthy visits more bearable.

Registration hasn't started yet because the charts are still locked in the back office where I left them yesterday. Hurrying over to the main building in search of the key, I retrieve it from a midwife attending to a labouring mother in the maternity ward, and scurry back. As Masika and I lug the baskets up to the front, I give her a quick tutorial, even as patients clamour around us.

'Masika, all of the men's charts are in this blue basket. You take it,' I tell her. 'They're arranged in alphabetical order by last name. The women are in the green one and the children are in the red. I'll give those out.' I stop to catch my breath before continuing, 'Tell the men to come to you and the women to me.' As Masika begins to shout over raised voices to give directions, a man shoves his right hand into the green basket in front of me.

'*Bbaa.*' I point to Masika's basket. '*Busaasa ara Masika*', I say, signalling that men's charts are with her. He reaches across my basket and dives into the blue one. A stout woman with thick braids squeezes up beside him, speaking rapidly and trying to rummage around in the basket in front of me. I'm unable to follow her Lubwisi but hold up my hand. When she stops talking, I ask what her name is. Then, I sift through the women's charts and locate hers in a few seconds.

Next up is Topi, my favourite patient. She's easy to spot in the same maroon skirt and navy and white polyester top she wears at each visit. Wrapped around her waist is a faded *kitenge* which straps her eighteen-month-old son to her back. She's not twenty yet but because of the virus replicating in her blood, she looks like she's in her mid-fifties and has had a hard life. A fringe crowns her forehead from her mop of straightened hair. As she pushes forward towards me, I notice that when the others see her, they move away.

'*Olaayo*, Topi,' I say, smiling and handing over charts for herself and her son. Nodding and taking the blue folders, she looks at me with a haunting expression, her bulging eyes peering out from above her hollowed-out cheeks. As she turns to go and get weighed, a large man with a full face says something to her, saliva spraying. A young woman with him snickers. Topi keeps moving. Watching her take measured, determined steps towards the scales, I notice her son's head resting between her protruding shoulder blades.

I lean across to Masika. 'What did that man say to Topi?'

'He asked, "Why do you come here to get drugs? We can tell you're not taking the medicine."' I feel heat rise at the roots of my hair. I don't doubt that Topi is taking her antiretrovirals but she could be one of those for whom these life-extending drugs are no longer effective. This clinic is one of the only places in this community where the stigma of living with HIV is absent, yet these fellow sufferers have chosen to alienate Topi. I wonder if it's because her appearance reminds them of the likelihood of their own shortened lives.

It takes lots of repetition and correction for the patients to understand that I'm giving out charts for women and children, and Masika is doing the same for men, but eventually they start to get the idea. When things quieten down for a few moments, I look over at what Masika's doing. For each patient, she's sifting through charts ten at a time, lifting them out to continue looking, creating a new pile and undoing all the work I put in yesterday.

'Masika, you don't have to start at the top. They're in order.'

'Aren't all the ones for men here?'

'Yes, but they follow the alphabet. The one for Birungi is near the top. The one for Kyalimpa is close to the middle, like A, B, C, D. Keep them in the same order; otherwise it doesn't work.' I move over to show her. She stares at me, uncomprehending. I try again. She hangs her head.

'Pam.Ella, let me find it myself.' With patients still trickling in and reaching across the table in front of us for their charts, I realise this is not the time to teach something new. Though tempted to insist, I hold my tongue and go back to my baskets, leaving Masika to sift through charts in her own way.

Perhaps I can salvage this new system when we're putting the charts back, I reason to myself. But things don't improve. Try as I might to rearrange the charts as patients leave, all I can manage is to remind the counsellor and the midwife who've joined us, that there are three different baskets, and they're labelled in both Lubwisi and English. At the end of a long morning, when Masika and I haul the baskets to the back office, I sigh. Children's charts are mixed in with the men's and those for women are dumped in with the children's.

So it has been for me to be back in Bundibugyo: familiar but at times frustrating. After a morning like this one, I find myself questioning why I ever returned. I've told people I came back to help support the Kwejuna Project's expansion and relieve Scott of shouldering this all himself. Given his other responsibilities as physician and team leader, I could see he was juggling many demands. Besides, he invited me to return, and that made me feel valued.

What's also true, however, is that I've come back to Bundibugyo for me. One main reason I came back was to gain more exposure to global health. Though humbled to be able to assist again with HIV prevention, because of the vastness of needs and the dearth of staff here, I may have the chance to learn more about malnutrition and infant mortality, perhaps see some surgery, or even encounter something new.

I also returned, not for selfish or ambitious reasons, but in a curious let-me-explore-this-more kind of way. With neither a job nor family to keep me in New York, I had the freedom to return. So, I have. After fifteen years of enduring the frenzied nature of the concrete jungle of the Big Apple, I discovered that my soul was ready to embrace the gentle pace and beauty of this slice of rural Africa, where lingering over conversations and receiving unexpected visitors are the norm. Despite the many hardships of my first stint here, including these very adjustments, I tasted something different and want to savour that more. I also want an extended experience of living and working in a community alongside others, though I know it will stretch me, far more than I can anticipate.

At times it feels like I never left, though I've been gone for a year. Besides Scott and Jennifer, other teammates like Michael and Karen and their children are all still here, and I'm living with Pat in the duplex again. Turns out Robinah is no longer in Bundibugyo. Having completed O levels, she's gone to Kampala for advanced study in preparation for university.

Other changes exist at almost every turn, however, and some adjustments are wearisome as well as welcome. Several fun-loving young women, here to teach the missionary kids, have replaced Bethany on the other side of the duplex. I'm enjoying getting to know them. At the same time, I find absorbing the rhythm, schedules and extra visitors brought on by these additional people all living under one roof to be a significant challenge. While I function well around people, I need a lot of time without others to recharge and replenish. I love being at home by myself, especially when it's by choice. In a village culture such as this, where Ugandans place a huge value on relationships and visiting, and being on a team who cherish life together, I'm all the more desperate to protect my solitude. With four of us in adjoining dwellings and two houseworkers here during the day, time alone is rare. Fortunately, this set-up is temporary. These teachers will move to the house next door in May when another teammate leaves, and I will shift to the other side of the duplex and have my own place.

Another thing that's different is that Dr Jonah is back. Having heard a lot about Jonah – the friend of Scott and Jennifer's who's now finished his medical training – when I first came, I'm eager to meet him. Hopefully soon.

# 16
## The Lesson

I find Jesika sitting in front of her home, a simple dwelling with a zinc roof. Her two daughters, still too young for school, are drawing pictures on the ground at her feet. An older woman with smooth, dark skin, who bears a resemblance to Winnie Mandela, is sprawled out on a mat beside them. Jesika offers me a stool and introduces me to her mother. After we all exchange greetings, Jesika disappears inside. Her mother and I smile at each other but sit in silence, not knowing what else to say.

I'm here for my first language lesson. This time around in Bundibugyo I want to make a real effort to learn to speak Lubwisi. Pat has suggested I work with her close friend Jesika because she's a confident English speaker and very sociable. As I wait for Jesika and listen to the girls chatting with each other, straining to pick up any words I recognise, a crowd cheers, then groans and a whistle blows. Looking in the direction of the excitement through the barbed wire and between jackfruit trees swollen with large green melons, I spot a match being played on a football field. I didn't realise it at first, but from this angle, I see that Jesika's yard borders the Christ School compound. Craning my neck to the left, I make out the home of the Barts, Kevin and JD, who started the school ten years ago.

'You ready?' Jesika asks, returning with a scarf covering her short hair. I hesitate. *'Tu gende,'* Jesika insists. 'We go. I going to take you around. You talk to people.'

Walking away from the direction of the school and following a narrow path hidden between several homes near Jesika's, we encounter two women. They're leaning against a simple whitewashed house with a door that's ajar; there's a charcoal fire smouldering beside them. One has a basin on her lap. Piled beside her are bunches of spinach-like leaves and stalks. She's discarding the stems and putting the leaves into the basin. The mortar next to her suggests she's preparing *sombe*, pounded cassava leaves which are boiled and flavoured with salt.

The other woman is yanking rough brown skin off cassava tubers. Steam is escaping from a fire-stained pot of boiling water balancing on three stones. As we approach, the cassava peeler smiles, revealing a gap in her teeth, and gets up to retrieve a stool and a wooden chair from under a tree. Jesika takes the stool. They insist I sit on the chair. Jesika begins by greeting them. I follow with: *'Mulaayo. Mulimutia?'*

*'Turio,'* they respond. It is well. Jesika speaks again. I hear the word 'Lubwisi' and they look at me with renewed interest. I grin, aware they'll soon discover how little I know. I start off with the few questions I've learned to use with women at the clinic.

*'Baliye bwawe aliyo?'* I ask the woman preparing the *sombe*. Most women are married here but I don't see a man around.

*'Talliyo ba, agendiye mukatale.'* She tells me her husband has gone to the market.

*'Nangaki?'* I ask, wondering why.

*'Agendiye bicoles.'* He's gone to get beans. I smile.

Turning to the other woman, I ask about children.

*'Orina baana banga?'*

*'Sie? Esatu.'* She holds up three fingers even though I've understood her, and then turns the question on me.

Jesika bursts out laughing, rolling her head back with glee. I shake my head, playing along with this inside joke. I'm quite sure this woman knows I don't have any children. Though I've not met them before and haven't been back long, in this small community, where news travels fast, the Ugandans tend to pay keen attention to the basics about outsiders.

'*Nangaki?*' Now it's her turn to ask me why not.

'Jesika, tell them. I don't have a husband.'

Jesika translates and the woman responds.

'She's saying you don't need a husband to have children.' I smile and shake my head. The women keep speaking. It starts to go back and forth and then speeds up.

Unable to make out where the conversation is going, I decide to jump in. 'Jesika, what are you saying? I don't understand.'

'The other woman says maybe you don't have a husband because you can't speak Lubwisi. It's so easy to learn. See how well even the children speak it.' I try to laugh this off, but it stings. I wish it were that simple. I've had a fantastic life being single but in all honesty it's not something I expected at this stage. Still, I can't say I haven't had my chances.

The bantering between Jesika and the women continues. I place a smile on my face, but feel disconnected from the conversation. Suddenly, the tone shifts and Jesika laughs. I tune in again.

'She wants you to marry her son!' Jesika exclaims, chuckling some more.

'*Bbaa,*' I respond. No.

'*Nangaki?*' Why not?

'*Bbaa nawe,*' I repeat, shaking my head. No way. They laugh and I join them, grateful for a gracious way to re-engage. As the giggling continues, I grab Jesika by the arm.

'I've had enough for the first day,' I tell her. She follows my lead and gets up. We say goodbye, smile and wave, retracing the path back to Jesika's.

At her place, I thank her. '*Weebale,* Jesika, thank you, that was good, but next time, please let's go more slowly.'

'Yes, next time,' she agrees.

Strolling home along the main road, with dusk approaching and shadows elongating, I muse about how difficult language learning will be and how uncomfortable it is not knowing Lubwisi. At least in Jos, though my Hausa-speaking remains very basic, I've come to have a decent understanding of quite a lot that's being said, and that is helpful. Will I ever really learn what people are saying here? Or will I constantly feel like an outsider? I muse again about why I returned. Why am I putting myself through this? I didn't have to come back. I made a choice to. A complicated choice, yes, but a choice nonetheless.

Yet, at the end of the day, if I'm really honest with myself, despite all the reasons I've put forward, ultimately I came back because God called me back here. He created the clear opportunity, gave me enough of a desire to return, and provided the funds through the generosity of family, friends and other supporters. I know it will be hard. After all, those first three months were really hard too. I just hope this time around it'll be less challenging. I'm not as naïve and feel more prepared for whatever I'll face.

It's almost dark when I get back to the duplex. Sauntering up the driveway, eager for dinner, I notice a motorcycle parked under the mango tree. Hearing voices and laughter coming from inside, I hesitate for a few moments. Not in the mood to be sociable, I'm tempted to go around to the back, but that seems silly. And cowardly. So, bolstering my emotions, I walk up to the door, pull back the curtain of our greeting room and step inside.

Pat is there, seated next to a dark, stocky man. His whole face is lit up as if he's just shared a private joke with her. When he sees me, he stands and I notice we're about the same height, about five feet five inches.

Grabbing and squeezing my hand, he bursts out with, 'Hello, Pam, I'm Jonah. I've been wanting to meet you.'

'Oh, so you're Dr Jonah,' I say, my mood lifting. 'Please, please sit.' As I join him on the bench, Pat gets up and excuses herself. 'Scott and Jennifer told me you were back. I know they're very proud of you, the first doctor to come from Bundibugyo in twenty-nine years!'

'We've become good friends,' Jonah says, smiling, his cheeks turning chubby. 'And our families. We have five children, all girls. They have four. We've eaten many meals together.' He beams again. 'They've supported me so much. They helped with the fees for medical school and people in their church bought me textbooks. It wasn't easy. I had reached more than thirty by then, and Mellen and I had already started having the children.'

'But by God's grace, you made it. They told me you could have got a good job in Kampala when you finished.'

He nods. 'There were some offers, yes, but I had to come back.'

'How is it, being back?'

'Well, it's been some time since we lived here, about seven years. The small ones are fine, but our two oldest daughters are still adjusting,' he chuckles. 'They're used to lights, a fridge, even TV. We have a nice TV in our Kampala house,' he tells me, his eyes glistening.

'You have a house there?'

'Yes, we kept the house. The older girls will go back to school next month. The third one will join them next year. My mother stays there with them.'

'Are you glad to be back?'

'Very happy. Of course, my family is from here. What about you? How are you finding Bundibugyo? Scott told me you were here before.'

'I came for a few months last year. He asked me to come back to help with Kwejuna.' Steering the conversation back to Jonah, I ask, 'Are you at Nyahuka?'

'I've not been posted yet. The Ministry would like me at Bundibugyo Hospital. I'm trying to change that. I want to be at Nyahuka.'

'Why would they post you to the hospital when Nyahuka has no medical director?'

Frowning, his upbeat mood deflates. 'Nyahuka makes more sense. I was there before, but things are sometimes political, you know.' He flashes me a knowing look, then recovers quickly. 'We'll see what happens. Anyway, I just wanted to say hello. Nice to meet you, Pam.' He extends his right hand. 'See you soon.' I follow him outside.

After he starts his motorcycle and drives off, I head in for dinner, touched by his friendliness and hopeful he'll get posted to the health centre down the road.

# 17
# The Visitors

Jennifer rushed back to Virginia two weeks ago with her three youngest children. Her father's health had begun to decline. Scott and Luke followed a week later. Once again, they've left me in charge. Kwejuna has grown to seven sites from the original two, there are now eighty-five staff involved, and the administrative and reporting requirements have multiplied too. Having been back for less than two months, overseeing a project that's grown to this size and scope is daunting, particularly as I'm still finding my way as the assistant director.

Fortunately, weekly Thursday meetings and pizza nights have continued. These times with the team are a welcome respite from the many demands. Since Scott left, Michael has taken over at the outdoor oven.

'Now that we're done eating, let's start cleaning up,' he yells out. 'But before the movie, I'm going to tell you about the call I had with Scott today.'

That's great news. When Scott left, he planned to be back in a month. I can't wait for that. Visiting all the sites on a regular basis is far more challenging without him. Most are a few kilometres away, but two are several hours away going towards Fort Portal, requiring a sturdy vehicle, which I don't have. I could get to most of the other clinics by motorcycle, but relying on these taxis daily isn't practical in the long run, or affordable.

Scott and I talked about me getting a motorcycle, but due to a bureaucratic delay with the grant, it isn't here yet.

Then, because of how large the programme has become, when I do get to the newer sites by riding with Joseph, who's still providing administrative support, or when I hire the occasional motorcycle taxi, recognising the Kwejuna staff and remembering their names remains a stretch for me. There are of course many more monthly reports to complete for the Ministry of Health now too. Getting the data is often a mad scramble because it's in multiple registers in different locations at each facility. Joseph and I share this task, but for the sites that are hard to visit, we've deferred to making calls and cajoling the staff there to scour all the relevant sources. As if all of this wasn't already a lot to manage, staff from the foundation which supports our work are eager to visit the programme. I'm counting on Scott being back in time to host them.

Eager to hear about Michael's conversation with Scott, I rush around with the others, dumping dirty plates into a basin. We chuck empty soda bottles into crates and toss leftover pizza slices into plastic containers. As we lug chairs back into the living room, the children are hurling pillows at one another.

'Kids, please don't do that inside,' says Karen. 'The movie will be starting soon. Come and sit down.' Raising her voice to move things along, she calls out to her husband, 'Michael, we're ready in here.' Full and satisfied, I plop down on one of the wicker chairs. Michael soon joins us.

'Great pizza tonight, if I say so myself,' he smirks, looking around the room. Then, his tone shifts. 'Spoke to Scott today.' He pauses. 'Jennifer's dad's getting worse. He's having trouble eating.' Michael adjusts his glasses before continuing. 'He now needs help dressing and going to the bathroom. Soon he'll have to be fed through a tube.' My mind is whirling as I try to absorb these sobering details. He goes on, 'This is really hard for them. It's also not a surprise. It's the nature of ALS. His muscles will only get weaker.'

I can't imagine what it's like for Jennifer to see her father slowly approaching paralysis. Their family circumstances sadden me, but as Michael's been talking, I remain anxious about the upcoming site visit. No surprise, I've not been sleeping well since I found out about it.

'What are Scott's plans?' I ask. 'When's he coming back?'

Michael takes a little too long to respond, but I remain optimistic.

'Scott really feels he should stay.' Michael hesitates, stroking his goatee. 'Jennifer needs him, and it makes sense for the family to be together right now.' He's quiet. I wait, still hoping. 'He doesn't know when he'll be back, but feels he should stay until the end. That will probably happen in the next couple of months.'

No one says anything. I stare at my hands in my lap and fidget with them. My stomach does a flip. I want Scott back, if not next week, then the one after. I understand his desire and need to be with his family. Of course, that makes sense. Especially in these circumstances. At the same time, I'm in over my head. How am I going to cope with this site visit?

Michael interrupts my thoughts. 'Until they come back, Karen and I will continue to be team leaders. As for Kwejuna, Scott's very confident that it's in good hands with you, Pamela.' I feel his eyes on me, so I look up but say nothing.

Learning about Scott's decision is disappointing, more so than I want to admit. I don't want to have to host people from Kampala that I've never met and hardly spoken to. I'd been clinging to the hope that Scott would return soon. I really, really don't want to be the person in charge of Kwejuna, again. Yet, I'm learning more and more that a life lived with God is not about what I want. And, I am trying to live less selfishly. Being on a team is like being in a family, I'm discovering. There's a constant need for give and take, and always others and a greater good to consider. Still, knowing these things in my head doesn't mean it isn't hard to deal with. Having been in this situation before, it's as if my iPod is jammed, stuck on the same song, unable to move to the next one in my playlist. I knew when I came back that Scott and Jennifer would leave again to be with her father. I just didn't think it would happen so soon. And when he left, Scott told me he'd be back shortly.

The kids begin to squirm, eager for the movie to begin. Pat stays behind, but I skip it, desperate to be on my own. As I walk back to the duplex, stumbling through the dark, a dog howls in the distance and tears spill onto my cheeks.

I can't avoid it. Scott or no Scott, the site visit will go ahead and I will have to stand in for him. Two public health doctors from EGPAF's office in Kampala will be here next week observing the programme. Named after Elizabeth, the wife of the seventies' actor Paul Michael Glaser, who contracted HIV from a blood transfusion and passed it on to two of their kids, the foundation's mission is to end AIDS in children.[1]

I dread site visits. They remind me of my first one as director of the Bronx when I'd only been in the job a few months. Eager to impress those funders, before they arrived I reviewed every page in every file to make sure our paperwork was flawless. They were impressed, but it wasn't sufficient. When they failed to appreciate how challenging it was to engage poor women in clinical trials and zeroed in on our mediocre retention rates, I fought to defend our efforts. Along with my boss, we did our best to advocate for our participants and tried to get our visitors to understand the many challenges these marginalised women faced. They eventually backed off, but the experience left me disheartened and cautious. Whenever those financially supporting the work wanted to visit, I'd learned to put my guard up.

Dr William, the foundation's national director, and Dr Miriam, his colleague, arrive in Bundibugyo on a Monday afternoon. After warm introductions, cold soft drinks, and a hearty lunch, Pat and I take them to Kakuka, a small facility in the mountains near the Democratic Republic of the Congo.

They've come prepared. William, a stocky man with a slight moustache and a shaved head, is wearing khakis and hiking boots. Miriam, in her mid-thirties with short straightened hair, looks ready for a mountain climb herself. Tall and impressive, she's in a pair of jeans. I soon discover Miriam is armed with lots of questions.

Kakuka is one of the newer sites so I'm less familiar with the staff. The midwife and lab technician appear hard-working, but I have not yet met the clinical officer who's in charge, something I feel uneasy about. After touring the facility, we gather in the small waiting room. It's late in the day so the pregnant women are long gone, but the air is warm and stifling. Miriam begins by asking the staff about how many women they're seeing for prenatal visits and what the monthly HIV testing rates are.

The midwife and lab tech respond, but the third person, a man, thirtyish, whom I've never met, dressed in slacks, a long-sleeved shirt and a tie, appears interested but says nothing. During a lull in the discussion, Miriam turns to him.

'Are you the in-charge?' He nods his head. I sit up and take a renewed interest in him. 'How many staff here are involved in Kwejuna?' she asks.

He appears not to have understood the question. A vacant look is on his face. In the silence, the midwife butts in. 'He's a nursing assistant who does the HIV counselling.'

'I thought you were the in-charge?' Miriam challenges, looking at him and then at me.

'I've not met the in-charge,' I explain in a soft voice, blood rushing to my cheeks. 'Whenever I've come, he's not been around.' It's true but as I say it, it sounds pathetic.

Miriam frowns and the awkwardness passes, but I feel my defences rising. Despite the size of the burgeoning programme, being unable to identify an employee hints at incompetence. How can I supervise people well if I don't know those I'm supposed to be overseeing? This is a minor incident, I know, but since it occurs so early in the visit, it puts me on edge. I wonder when the next gaffe will come.

It doesn't take long.

On day two, we go to the prenatal clinic at Bundibugyo Hospital, which Scott brought me to in my first week. That was fifteen months ago. This time, I'm the one ushering our guests around. The waiting room is packed with women, their bellies swollen to various sizes. Voices, laughter and babies crying meet us when we enter. A midwife, dressed in her white uniform with the sun-yellow Kwejuna project logo emblazoned on her right sleeve, is addressing a group, gesturing with her hands.

Slim, dark and in her late twenties, Anna is delivering HIV education in Lubwisi. In the US or UK, one makes an individual decision to be counselled and tested before receiving information about the disease or the test, but here the reverse occurs. After explaining what HIV is, how it is transmitted and why they should be tested, Anna will offer them all an HIV test. Those who don't want to be tested can refuse or opt out. Few do.

Because none of us understand what Anna is saying, we watch as the women listen and nod their heads. Then, she appears to direct them to line up outside a small room adjacent to the waiting area. They crowd into a dark corridor, forming a jagged procession. We follow them to the makeshift lab. The first woman, with wide hips, a bump on her stomach and a baby asleep on her back, trudges in, sits and gives her pink prenatal card to the lab technician. He documents her card number and pulls out a test strip, then jabs her middle finger with a lancet and draws blood. She winces. I wince too. Smearing the drop on the strip, he sets it aside. Without waiting for the result, the woman saunters back towards the waiting room. The whole procedure takes less than thirty seconds.

'Once the tech records the results, he'll take the cards to Anna,' I explain. 'Only those who are positive will meet with her one-on-one.'

'Why don't the midwives do the finger stick?' asks Miriam. 'It would be more efficient.'

I offer what I think is a logical response. 'Using a midwife would slow down the visits.'

Miriam counters with, 'A nursing assistant could record the results. You don't need a midwife to do that. At other sites, midwives do the finger sticks.'

'They're not trained,' I explain.

'No problem. We can send yours to Fort Portal for training.'

I try to push back. 'We have about 100 patients today. We've set up this lab here so we don't have to send them over to the main lab. That would make the visits much longer. Some might not come back.'

'We've seen midwives involved in testing at some of our other health centres. It provides uninterrupted care.'

I try to push back once more. 'Am not sure how that would work for us. This tech also tests those who come in voluntarily for HIV testing.'

'You may have a good system but using your midwives more is something we want you to rethink. Consider it professional development,' insists Miriam.

'We'll look into it,' I concede, anticipating how challenging this will be. I know from Scott that some in this clinic already resent the extra work they've taken on, counselling and testing pregnant mothers. He is well loved and has a much longer track record here than I do, so perhaps he can persuade them to take on more. I pull out a notebook and jot down this suggestion for him.

The site visit continues to stretch me.

That afternoon, we go to another, smaller, health facility, Busaru. As she did on Monday, Miriam quizzes the staff about the numbers of women who were counselled and tested in February. We pull out the register and review the data.

'How do these numbers compare to previous months?' She looks at me for an answer.

'That would be clear from a quarterly review, but with this being the first week of March, we haven't had a chance to compile the first quarter's data yet.'

Shrugging her shoulders, she says, 'It would be helpful to see the most up-to-date monthly data as we visit each site.'

'We normally would have done that by now but because of the site visit, we spent time preparing instead,' I explain.

'I understand,' Miriam tells me, 'but when can you get us a report? It would be helpful to us this week.'

'We'd need a couple of days.' My shoulders tighten. Even a couple of days would be near impossible. Joseph would have to scramble to gather this data from all the sites on his own.

'OK, try by Thursday,' Miriam confirms.

I give her a half-hearted nod.

Responding to all the questions about why we do what we do, especially when I'm not always sure, and working out how to gather data that's not quick to collect becomes tiring. By the end of only the second day, frazzled and drained because I've been with our visitors the whole time and talking almost non-stop without a break, my introverted self has had little time to decompress. I'm already eager for the visit to end. My sleep has been terrible too. I eventually learned to relax during site visits in the Bronx, but at night during this one, my mind is lurching from one anxious thought to another.

On Wednesday morning, sluggish, and hopeful that my glasses will obscure my reddened eyes, I take our guests to the prenatal clinic at Nyahuka. Though Nyahuka is the site I'm most familiar with, our visitors manage to probe things I can't answer: 'Why don't you have different receptacles for dry and wet kinds of waste in each clinic?' Sounds reasonable and we can implement this, though it's not something I realised was a requirement. 'Why are you using your own register instead of the three the Ministry provides?' There must be a sound reason why Scott has chosen to create our own register, but I don't know what it is. After digging around in the Kwejuna office, the government registers surface, covered in dust. I add both of these issues to my list to discuss with Scott.

The biggest request comes after lunch.

'We want all of our sites to begin testing for T-cell counts,' Miriam tells me, 'so your clinical officers can more accurately assess how advanced your mothers' HIV disease is.'

I try to resist gracefully. 'We'd love to do that here in Bundibugyo, but with no electricity, those tests would have to be done in Fort Portal.'

'We know. There's a large regional referral hospital there that could do them.'

I hesitate before trying to explain our situation. 'The challenge for us is getting the blood to Fort Portal. There's no refrigeration here.'

'I'm sure you can make arrangements,' Miriam says, enthusiastically. I don't disagree with her. I also don't relish organising how to get tubes of blood to remain refrigerated and safe for three hours in thirty-four degree temperatures over a rocky never-been-paved road. A dull headache that's been lurking threatens to take hold. I open my notebook and add this to my list for Scott.

On Thursday afternoon, William and Miriam conclude their visit a day early. Grateful and relieved, I invite them to join us for pizza that evening. It's a light-hearted and enjoyable occasion. We part on friendly terms, but by the time they pull out early on Friday, I'm exhausted. The week has been like a climb through the Rwenzoris with expert mountaineers. While I was out of shape and lacking stamina, they were in top condition and familiar with the terrain. I spend the weekend recovering, nursing not just sore muscles but a fragile ego.

The encounter with these competent physicians has exposed my over-desire to be capable, intelligent and impressive. But, instead of coming across as someone with a firm grasp of Kwejuna, I've felt half a step behind, confronting operational questions I couldn't answer, and challenged to add more tasks to staff that are already at full capacity.

Now, on Sunday evening, reflecting on all that transpired during the week and after spending some time naming my fears, praying through them, and exploring reasons for my resistance to Miriam's input, I've realised the site visit, though difficult, was not as much of a disaster as I'd thought. I can see that Miriam really was trying to help us improve how Kwejuna functions and this was in fact an integral part of her role as a representative of the foundation that funds our work. From this vantage point, I'm much more able to value her and William's partnership, and I know Scott does too.

That being said, and though my sense of self has been restored, it doesn't change the fact that I remain eager for Scott to return.

# 18
# The Discovery

Jennifer's father passed away in Virginia during the early hours of Easter Monday. After they bury him, and take some weeks to grieve, we meet up with Scott, Jennifer and their children at a conference in Greece and then all return to Bundibugyo at the end of May.

Ten days after we get back, the motorcycles that Scott had written into the renewal grant – one each for Joseph and me – turn up. Following months of delays, the foundation cleared our Yamaha AG 100s through customs, registered them and gave them Ministry of Health number plates. Then they were strapped to the back of a pick-up truck and driven seven hours across the country to Bundibugyo Town. Joseph collected his there and agreed to ride mine to the mission.

'Yes, that's Joseph,' Scott confirms, looking out through the screened windows which face their front yard. A motorcycle has just pulled into their compound and gone silent. 'We can review numbers at our next meeting. Let's go and see your machine,' he says, clapping his hands.

My hands, in contrast to his, begin to get clammy at the thought of that motorcycle. Even though I've overcome my initial anxiety about *boda bodas*, the five-month delay in getting my own machine has left me questioning whether I really need one here. I ride with Pat or Scott to the hospital on Fridays, and Joseph has been taking me to the other health centres on an old motorcycle he's been borrowing. Jonah, who's based at the hospital but is still hoping to get posted to Nyahuka, gives me a lift now and then too, which is great as I don't see him as much as I'd like to. Those rides give us a chance to catch up. But having never been much of a car driver, I'm no longer that keen to learn to ride a motorcycle. Wiping my palms on my dress, I follow Scott, who's already on his way outside.

My first ever vehicle is shiny and blood red. The petrol tank, complete with a shimmering silver cap, sits in front of a wide black leather seat. A sturdy rack is bolted on behind. Though striking in a place where so few things are brand new, and dare I even say beautiful, the motorcycle is large and imposing.

'Do you want to see what it feels like?' Scott asks. Not really. My heart is thumping, but because I want to appear brave, I grab hold of the black rubber handles and mount the bike. As I ease myself down on the seat, I make sure the hem of my dress is grazing my mid-calves. Then, firmly grasping the handlebar on the right, I plant my feet on the ground and push the kickstand back with my right foot, but I quickly find myself unable to bear the machine's weight. I grip the bars more tightly, trying to keep the motorcycle upright. Still, it begins to topple beneath me. Grimacing, my lips pressed together, my knuckles straining, I lean forward and manage to stop the slide. The motorcycle has just taught me my first lesson. It may look like an oversize bicycle but it must weigh at least 100 kilos, nearly twice as much as I do.

'I didn't realise it would be so heavy,' I say, wiping my face with the back of my hand.

'It's solid, isn't it? Want me to show you how to start it?' Scott asks.

'Uh – no, why don't you try it out?' I dismount in a hurry and Scott and I change places. He climbs on with ease.

'This is nice. Brand new. Less than twenty kilometres!' he says, staring at the odometer. 'Looks like it made it from Kampala in great shape.'

'Yes, not bad,' Joseph agrees. 'Much better than the one I've been using.'

'For sure.' Scott presses his foot down on the starter pedal. After several attempts, the machine purrs. 'Get on, Pamela, I'll take you home.'

'That's OK,' I say, stepping back. 'I've got my bike with me. I'll ride it over.'

'All right. Joseph, wait here for me.'

When I get to the duplex, where I'm now living across from Pat, I find the motorcycle parked next to my front door under the shade of a slight, wispy tree with small yellow flowers. Looking at the machine and knowing it's mine, for the first time, a burst of pride surges inside me. My fingertips even get tingly. But as I inspect my new possession, I realise I have a problem. I'll need to bring it inside overnight.

But how to get it in there? Even though there's only one step up into the greeting room, the motorcycle is far too heavy for me to lift. How will I manage this every day? No idea. Lesson number two: owning a vehicle, like possessing anything, brings unanticipated responsibilities. I walk around my machine, marvelling at its newness while pondering what to do. The tingling in my fingers has crept up to my shoulders and doesn't feel so good. What to do? Leaving the motorcycle parked where Scott left it, I take the keys out of the ignition and go inside to make lunch.

That afternoon, I call Michael. As an engineer, he seems able to fix and do most things.

'My motorcycle arrived this morning,' I tell him, pacing around in the driveway where the signal's stronger.

'At last. You ready to begin lessons?'

'Not yet. Right now, I'm just trying to figure out where to park it at night.'

'I wouldn't leave it outside,' he says. 'What about the greeting room?'

'I thought of that, but it's too heavy. I can't lift it.'

'You could get a ramp made,' Michael suggests.

'A ramp? I never thought of that.' I turn and look at my front step. 'Can you do it?'

'Sure, but you should ask Benjamin. He'd be glad for the extra money.' Michael gives me Benjamin's number, and within twenty minutes, a man with a wiry frame and pencil-thin moustache is at my front door. Over the next hour, he buys a bag of cement from the market, hauls it up the road on a *boda boda*, mixes it, plasters a smooth ramp at the base of my front door, and takes the leftovers as a bonus.

When the cement dries, I rearrange the three armchairs in my greeting room to create an empty space alongside the bench. Then I attempt to heave the motorcycle up the incline. Even with the ramp, the task is daunting. The motorcycle is still far too heavy for me and now I'm working against its weight. Utilising the brake, I manage to edge it gingerly up the ramp, the muscles in my forearms twitching. As I get closer to the top of the slope, it feels heavier and heavier until I can't move it any more. It begins to slide backwards. I throw my body towards the door, clamping down hard on the handbrake. I stop and try to regroup. Then, slowly, I release the brake ever so slightly and centimetre by centimetre, I nudge the machine upwards, straining to overpower it. It's a painstaking task, two steps forward, one step back. Eventually, the front wheel rolls half way in through the door, and then stops abruptly.

I don't believe it. The handlebars don't fit. To coax them in, I swivel them back and forth, alternating between the left and the right, then the right and the left, each time moving inside a little more. Though laborious, this eventually works, and once the handlebars are all the way in, the rest of the machine rolls in easily. The motorcycle comes to rest on the far right side of the room, with the soft chairs as its audience. It takes about a minute to get it inside, and my armpits are damp and my biceps ache.

The airstrip is the perfect place to learn how to ride, especially for someone as challenged as me. Though there are sometimes a few people walking along a path that meanders down the right side – usually women balancing vegetables from their gardens on their head – in this wide green expanse, there's no danger of me knocking anyone down or running into anything. The runway is a long and broad field, with elephant grass and banana trees clustered together at its edges, cheering me on. When I'm facing the road, the now familiar outline of the mountains beckons, majestic even on hazy days. When I'm riding in the other direction, the line where the horizon touches the airstrip stretches out before me, as if endless. During my better riding moments, I fantasise that I will just keep going and take off.

For the last two weeks, Michael has been picking me up on his machine in the afternoons and bringing me here for some basic lessons. I'm a slow learner and fearful, but his persistent reminders that I'm in control of what happens begin to sink in, and I come to believe him. Soon, I can putt along in a straight line down the centre of the airstrip. When I'm ready, he shows me how to make turns and do figures of eight, shifting my weight counter to the way the machine is tilting. As I become more relaxed cruising up and down, turning and increasing speed, Michael connects me with Godfrey, a young man who works with him, to teach me to ride my own motorcycle with him on the back.

The motorcycle lessons with Godfrey over a month pay off. Despite a shaky beginning, I can now manoeuvre the machine with him on the back, though I'm still a cautious driver. I'll keep using my bicycle to get around Nyahuka but will rely on my Yamaha to travel to some of the other health centres and when I go to the hospital on Fridays.

Today, for the first time, I'll be carrying Masika on the motorcycle. We're going to a health centre in Bubukwanga, five kilometres beyond Bundibugyo Town, where we'll spend the day with TBAs who've been begging me to come. Their leaders, whom I trained eighteen months ago now, have invited me to help them motivate the larger group to understand their role in

HIV prevention. We could take a taxi to town and then hire two *boda bodas*, but I'm eager to challenge myself to drive us all the way there on my motorcycle.

Masika meets me at the duplex around 8.30. To prepare for our ride, she straps the basket I've put my backpack in to the motorcycle rack, using a long piece of rubber made from an old tyre.

'What a good idea, Masika,' I tell her. 'That will give us more space.' However, I soon find that with both of us on the machine and the basket in place, it's a tight squeeze. When Masika tilts her head, her helmet bumps the back of mine. I have to arch my back and lean forward. I slide up until I'm almost on top of the petrol tank, but I can still feel Masika's thighs pressing into my back. I'm glad for my white tailor-made cotton capris; at least I don't have to be concerned about a dress getting in the way.

We edge down the driveway, the motorcycle's engine straining. I quickly discover Masika is much heavier than Godfrey. My knuckles white with anxiety, I remind myself, 'I can do this. I've carried Godfrey many times. This is just the same.'

We sputter out onto the main road and turn right. Accelerating, we ease past Jennifer and Scott's home, then the Church of Uganda, and after that a primary school. The machine begins to gather some speed. I loosen my grip on the handlebars and try to relax when we reach a blind hairpin curve. I slow down and we come around that corner without meeting any vehicles. We strain up a small hill and approach the airstrip. I power past it. Soon, we are cruising along at a steady pace.

Half way to Bundibugyo Town, fifteen minutes into our journey, we encounter a long, steep hill. I grip the handlebars tighter and shift to a lower gear. We start to climb but soon begin to lose speed. I press my foot on the pedal to accelerate. It makes no difference. We're not going fast enough. I realise too late that I've underestimated Masika's weight. Instead of speeding up, the motorcycle does the exact opposite of what

I'm trying to get it to do. It crawls. Before we reach the middle of the hill, the engine sputters, takes one last gasp and cuts off. When it dies, it starts to topple over. The weight is unmanageable. I can't hold us all up. I plant my left foot on the ground, fighting with the motorcycle to steady it. My glasses slither down my nose. Behind me, Masika tumbles off. When I look around, I see that by some miracle, she has landed on her feet.

'Masika, I am so sorry. Are you OK?'

Brushing dirt off her dress, she exudes calm. 'Pam.Ella. Don't mind, the road is bad.'

'Are you OK?' I ask again, adjusting my glasses.

'Let me walk to the top,' she says, pointing ahead. 'Pick me up from there.' I don't argue. The truth is this is not the first time I've stalled here, which of course I don't tell her. I struggled carrying Godfrey on this very hill – the one time we rode to town together – and the machine gasped here too, so I should have remembered to switch to a lower gear sooner. Watching her trudge up the hill, I wonder if we should have just hired motorcycles after all, but it's too late for that now. Removing my helmet, I wipe the sweat off my face and tousle my curls. I take my time strapping it back on. Then, praying for courage and trying not to beat myself up, I mount the machine and get my bearings. As soon as I start the engine, it comes alive and I ascend the hill with ease.

An hour after our mishap, with sore shoulders and sticky with sweat, we arrive in Bubukwanga. That we are so late is soon forgotten. Joseph is there to meet us and when we enter a large hall, forty lay midwives stand and cheer.

We begin with a short discussion about Kwejuna and the importance of testing pregnant mothers. I also do some teaching about HIV transmission and emphasise their role in referring women for prenatal care. When I ask for questions, a mature woman with a short afro begs me to issue them with IDs. For those times when they accompany a labouring mother to the hospital, they are often not recognised as legitimate healthcare workers and this is hurtful. Others murmur in agreement. I tell them I'll talk with Scott about their request. We finish our time together with rice and beans. Then Masika and I make our way back, this time with no incidents.

After dropping Masika off, I speed home, ignoring the shouts of '*Muzungu!*' from strangers on the road and '*Pam.Ella!*' from the children who recognise me. At the duplex, I bring the motorcycle inside, close my door, and collapse onto my bed. I'm in no hurry to go out again with Masika on my machine.

When I arrive at the HIV care clinic at Nyahuka the following Wednesday, still embarrassed about our mishap on the hill, it's hard for me to look Masika in the eye. Mercifully, she greets me as usual and doesn't bring it up.

The clinic feels chaotic today. The clerks are registering patients, but the waiting room is crowded and seems unusually disorganised. To help keep things moving, I move over to the kids' scales dangling by the window.

'Masika, let's ask the women with babies to line up over here.' Before she's finished making the announcement, a swell of mothers and infants begins to gather near us. I love holding little ones. In New York, I seldom interacted with kids. Here it's so different. Beautiful babies are everywhere and they're used to being held by all sorts of people, but they hate being weighed, and I don't blame them. Dangling naked in a large basket in front of a crowd of unfamiliar people isn't pleasant. Even if it lasts for only a few seconds, long enough for me to read the scale, most respond with a flood of tears.

During a lull, I notice a tiny woman in a yellow and green dress with a toddler wedged on her hip standing in the doorway. In the five months since I returned to Bundibugyo, I've never seen her before. Waving a blue chart in her hand, she approaches the scale. I greet her in Lubwisi but she stares at me, wordless. Taking her chart, I scan the name on it. My eyes move to the child. I know him. Beaming, I poke his belly. His eyes light up, but he's stingy with his smile. Today is no different.

'*Wabuchire*, Mustapha,' I say, speaking again to the woman who has brought him, this time in Lukonjo. She nods, peering up at me from a pair of melancholy eyes. Through Masika I learn she's brought her grandson to see Jennifer. Since Jennifer returned three weeks ago, each Wednesday after doing rounds on the ward, she stops in to see the children living with HIV. Mustapha, one of her favourites, has been here since the early days of this clinic. He's begun to gain weight at last, a huge encouragement.

I hold Mustapha while his grandmother peels off an olive-green T-shirt, soft fuzzy trousers and an old rag, damp with urine. He squirms when he's put into the swaying basket and belts out his customary cry. I glance at the scales and scribble down his weight. When I lift him out and hand him back, his tears revert to a few sniffles. After we dress him, I point to a bench where they can wait for Jennifer. Before she leaves, I ask Masika to find out where her daughter is today.

As they begin talking, the grandmother's eyes fill up. She shakes her head. The movement causes a tear to spill out. Topi must be gone. Watching her, my eyes threaten to get moist too.

It's almost 2.00 when I begin to head home. My bicycle has a flat tyre but I haven't had time to get it fixed. Since Nyahuka is so close and I'm still not eager to ride the motorcycle, I chose to walk. The afternoon temperature fatigues me and my skirt sticks to my legs. I amble back to the duplex, barely acknowledging the people I pass. My tummy growls, but the heaviness I feel about the news that Mustapha's mother has died eclipses my hunger, the long morning and even the sweltering sun. Topi had been little more than a skeleton for weeks now. At each visit, I wondered if it would be her last. Yet somehow, she seemed to be carrying on. Her determined will to live has left me unprepared for the grief welling up at the news of her passing. I've read the reports, seen the data and known for years that AIDS kills many of those who become infected – and that's more likely in places like this. Yet, she's the first patient I've known personally who's succumbed to the disease. I felt a deep affection for her. She was faithful in keeping her clinic appointments and seemed to be clinging tenaciously to life. Yet, without warning, death has now come very near.

At home, I down a cold glass of water. I nibble some cheese and crackers along with a cabbage salad for lunch, before I lie down, hoping to rest. My mind is a tangle of disconnected thoughts. I try to snooze, without success. Getting up an hour later, I sit down at my laptop, eager to ride on the information superhighway which will transport me out of this sad place for a few minutes. As my computer boots up, I glance at the clock only to realise I've missed my chance to go online. The one hour of internet time we have in the afternoons is over.

Listless, I click on the 'My Pictures' folder instead. The camera I brought with me has disappeared so I'm even more grateful now for the photos I have saved on my computer. I've had such a delightful time taking pictures of the children, the women and the mountains. The sunsets are spectacular too. I open up an early folder I created and look at images captured from almost two years ago. I see the ones I took my first time out on the motorcycles with Masika. I chuckle to myself when I remember her bargaining with our *boda boda* drivers that day at the taxi park and recall how nervous I was. Me and motorcycles have come a long way since then.

I come across the picture of that teenager we visited in Busunga. I gaze at it, paying attention to her body language. Though she agreed to pose, her stance was defiant. She glared at the camera. I touch the arrow on my keyboard to move on, but the expression in her eyes arrests me. I look at her again. I study her face. Then I realise she's conveying not anger but fear. She had seemed so vulnerable that day. Her husband, a soldier, had left her, and her baby was only four months old. I wondered if she resented the attention our visit might be causing her too.

I stare at her face again – really carefully. I've looked at this photo many times, but now I see something I'd not noticed before.

A cry escapes from my throat.

166

I can't believe it.

I know her.

I hadn't recognised her as a healthy sixteen-year-old.

But it's definitely Topi.

A young Mustapha, with his large soft curls, is nestled in her arms.

# 19
# The Demise

'Scott, the TBAs are asking for IDs. It came up at my training in Bubukwanga.' He and I are touching base during our weekly meeting.

'IDs?' he asks, looking out towards the road as a lorry rumbles past.

'They want recognition as health workers, with skills. They're convinced having identification will give them respect.'

'I can see why they want them, but we don't give out IDs.' I take a sip from my water bottle. Dry season has arrived and I'm thirstier than usual. 'We should leave that to the Ministry,' he continues. 'An ID from us could be interpreted as an endorsement.'

'Could we give them something else so they'd stand out? We gave those yellow Kwejuna T-shirts during the ambassador's visit, but that was more than two years ago. They're old now and I see lots of men wearing them too.'

'They were popular, weren't they?' he says grinning, his blue eyes gleaming.

'How about something else they could wear? Another T-shirt?'

Scott sits up. 'At one time, Jennifer thought of having aprons made for them, like a cover that they could slip over their clothes.'

'That's it!' I say, running with the idea. 'Let's make them aprons. I can see them. They could be one-size-fits-all, like a loose pinafore with ties on the side. What do you think?'

'That could work. They'd mark these TBAs as ones the mission trained, especially if we put our logo on them.'

'Great idea. We could make them royal blue, not pastel like the nurses' uniforms, so they'd look really different.' My mind is whirring. 'And how about a white pocket in front, with the logo, so they won't be easy to copy?'

Scott smiles, 'I think the TBAs will really like them.'

So, I set about trying to make a massive number of aprons. First, I have to work out how much material we'll need. I start with getting Rose, Masika's sister, who's a seamstress, to sew me a sample. I love what she comes up with: a one-size-fits-all blue pinafore. She tells me it took two metres. Based on that, we work out that 248 aprons will require five rolls of 100 metres. Being the businesswoman that she is, Rose, dark like Masika but a little taller and with glassy eyes, offers to go to Kampala to buy them, saving me the hassle of navigating that city's backstreets to buy the cloth wholesale. Returning three days later with the blue material, she makes white squares for the front pockets. When I get our logo silk-screened onto the squares via another quick trip to Kampala, Rose sews one on as a pocket. Our first apron looks beautiful.

Since I'm having such a large quantity made and the job will add up to a tidy sum of money, I want to spread the work between two tailors. I'd love to include at least one who's living with HIV. Rose is already involved, so I decide to go with her for half of them, but I have another tailor, Agnes' mother, in mind for the rest. Agnes, a quiet and hard-working student at Christ School, is in her third year. When I first met her in January, she asked me what I did. We were sitting in a hut with large open windows near the girls' dorm where she would often hang out in the afternoons.

'I work with Kwejuna,' I told her, 'helping mothers who have Slim not to pass it to their babies. You know Slim?' I asked, using the local name for AIDS. I may have seen a tear form before Agnes quickly brushed it away.

'Yes, I know it. My mother is in BAWILHA.' This was one of those rare times in Bundibugyo when someone told me they knew of a person living with HIV. Her mother was in a local AIDS support group for women.

'Does she work for them?' I asked, lowering my voice and leaning in closer to Agnes so that none of the other girls huddled nearby could overhear our conversation.

'No, she's a tailor, in Bundibugyo Town, but she goes to their meetings.'

'What's her name?'

'Maggie.'

'And your father?'

'He is late.'

'I'm so sorry.'

Agnes blinked, her eyes becoming watery again. Her courage in sharing her mother's status had stayed with me. Now that I can employ a widow living with HIV, I'm eager to do it. So, when I'm next in Bundibugyo Town, I'll try to locate Maggie.

On Friday, after spending the morning at the hospital's HIV clinic, I head into town. Turning off the main road, I follow the directions Agnes gave me and soon pull up beside a small storefront. The broad doorway reveals a modest shop with a counter and some shelves. Dismounting and removing my helmet, I hear the hum of a treadle sewing machine. As I approach the shop by stepping over a deep ditch, a woman seated behind the machine comes into view, her feet moving together in rhythm. A tape measure is dangling around her neck. Her face, which has delicate lips framed with short natural hair, is at once familiar. When she sees me, she stops sewing and offers me a bench.

'Are you Agnes' mother?'

'I'm the one,' she says, smiling.

'I'm Pam.Ella, from World Harvest.' I extend my right hand. 'Nice to meet you. Agnes told me you sew.' Maggie grins again. I take out the apron Rose made and show it to her.

'Can you make something like this?'

'Let me see.' She takes it from me. 'Yes, it's simple. No zip, no buttons.'

'How many metres will you need?'

She slides the tape measure off her shoulders and across the blue material.

'One should be enough, maybe one and one quarter.'

'One and a quarter metres? Is that all? And how much will you charge for each one?'

She holds up the apron again. '1,500.'

'1,500? Are you sure?' She's asking for about sixty pence.

'You want to give me less than that?' she asks, puzzled.

'No, no.' I reply hastily. 'It's a good price. Let's say 1,500.' Recovering, I add, 'I need to have more than 100 made. Can you do that?'

'Yes, please.'

'Great. Can you start with ten? I have some material here. I can bring you the rest next week. Is that OK?'

Riding back to the mission, the sun scorching the base of my neck and my hairline damp from the weight of my helmet, I redo the maths and work out that Rose is charging USh1,000 (about forty pence) more and using almost a whole extra metre for each apron than Maggie is. As I mull over how this is possible and feel annoyance rising in my chest, I get that sinking feeling that Rose has outwitted me.

I return to Bundibugyo Town the following Tuesday. It's another blistering day and the cicadas are humming louder than usual as I grind the motorcycle up that last bend to the top of the hill. Though it's not my main reason for coming to town, I stop at Maggie's to drop off the rest of the material. The ten aprons she's already finished, except for the missing white pockets, look flawless.

Then I make my way to the hospital to visit Jesika. I haven't seen much of her since I dropped my language lessons to take up the motorcycle. And because Pat is away in the US on a scheduled leave, Jesika has stopped coming round. However, rumours about her have been swirling like leaves being swept up by the wind and gathering momentum. John, who works in Pat's home, and Jesika both attend the same Church of Uganda. Some weeks ago, he told me Jesika had left her mother's house and her daughters, and moved in with a new husband. There was no wedding but when a woman moves in with a man here, that counts as a marriage. Yesterday, John mentioned that on Sunday he heard Jesika had been admitted to the hospital. I don't know why she's here or how serious it is, but I didn't want to wait to visit her until I'm here on Friday in case she's been discharged by then. I especially want to update Pat on Jesika's situation.

The women's ward, a nondescript space with grimy yellow walls, which time and dirt have aged, doesn't convey much of a sense of health or hope. A swirl of sweat, antiseptic and bleach punctuates the atmosphere. Wandering up and down the rows of narrow beds, I find Jesika towards the back on the left, her bed sheets in disarray. When I see her, I'm shaken. Her face is gaunt, her cheekbones pronounced and her arms appear bony. She must've dropped about fifteen kilos since I last saw her. Her eyes register recognition when she sees me, but she doesn't lift her head or attempt a smile. She manages to whisper a greeting, but it takes too much energy to say anything more. Her eyelids droop and close.

I turn to greet her husband, a chunky brown-skinned man with a shaved head, settled on a pillow by her head. We say hello in Lubwisi, but his face is blank, vacant. I doubt he has any idea who I am, much as I doubt this role reversal is what he expected when he took Jesika as his wife. A fork in his right hand tells me he may have been trying to coax Jesika to eat, without much success, it seems. An untouched plate of cassava and soup is by the bedside.

172

I stand there for a moment not sure what to do, as there's nowhere for me to sit. Then I see Jesika's *kitabo* on the bedside table. I point to it. Her husband hands me the blue notebook, its cover worn, the paper disintegrating. It smells as if it's been kept under a mattress. I open it, looking for clues about her condition. Turning several of the thin pages, my eyes scan the writing. It's barely legible. I hold the book closer and squint, trying to make out what's written there. I don't pick up much. I turn another page. Then another. And there, as I read the lines, I make out three letters. They signify a code I recognise.

I catch myself before I gasp.

Instead, I swallow hard. I wonder how long Jesika's been living with this virus now devastating her immune system. My eyes move from the *kitabo* to the shadow of the woman lying on the bed. I feel tears welling. I don't want to alarm Jesika's husband. He may not know of Jesika's diagnosis and it's not my place to disclose it. I steady my gaze and look at Jesika again, but don't trust myself to hold off much longer. Abruptly, I nod to her husband and walk unsteadily out of the ward into the glare of the sun.

'I went to visit Jesika today at the hospital,' I tell Pat on the phone that night.

'How is she?'

'Not good, not good at all.' I'm leaning against the back fence, inhaling the smell of cut grass. 'She recognised me but couldn't talk.' I press the phone right up to my ear. The line between North Carolina and Bundibugyo isn't very clear. 'She looked so thin it was shocking. Do you know why she's there?'

Pat's quiet for a moment. 'Why?' she asks. I notice she doesn't give a direct answer.

'I looked through her *kitabo*.' I suck in air, wondering how Pat will react. 'She's TRR.'

At first, Pat says nothing. Then, 'I know.'

'You know? What do you mean you know?' I feel indignation rising.

'She got tested at Nyahuka. One of the counsellors told me, but she's been living in denial.'

'How long have you known?' I suppress my disappointment.

'For a while. Before I left. I've felt bad knowing. The person who told me had broken confidentiality, but she wanted me to talk to her. I tried, many times. Tried to urge her to get treatment, but she wouldn't even talk about it.'

The phone starts to slip from my grasp, my ear slick with sweat.

'Sorry I couldn't tell you.' Pat's voice tapers off.

# 20

# The Doctor

I have no idea how to prepare for a Caesarean section in Bundibugyo. After splashing cold water on my face, I check that my new camera's inside my bag and sling it across my body. Minutes later I find myself on the back of Jonah's motorcycle. As we approach the health centre, my heartbeat is speeding up and the thud-thud-thud of blood pumping echoes in my ears. Jonah called moments ago, waking me from a lovely Sunday afternoon nap. Slow to answer the phone, I was groggy and disorientated, unsure at first if I was dreaming.

'Pam, this is Jonah. I'm on my way to Nyahuka. A woman with an obstructed labour needs a Caesar. Didn't you want to see one?'

I hesitate. 'Now?'

'The baby's in distress. We must go now. Am coming to pick you up.'

'OK.'

Click.

I've never witnessed any kind of surgery, but I considered becoming a medical doctor at one point, so I'm grateful for this opportunity. To observe Jonah performing a C-section is rarer than rain during the dry season. This C-section will be only the second one to occur at Nyahuka. Just a week before, Jonah christened the operating theatre with the first one, an emergency for the wife of a 'big man'. Until now, whenever C-sections were necessary, labouring mothers had to travel to Bundibugyo Hospital, something Jennifer told me when I first toured the health centre with her. The government-provided ambulance, a dilapidated white pick-up truck, is rarely on the road because it seldom has petrol, so heavily pregnant women have to settle for a jarring journey on the back of a *boda boda* if they don't secure the front seat of a pick-up taxi.

The absence of a government-employed doctor at Nyahuka to perform these life-saving operations has changed now that Jonah has returned. Here, he's not just well liked. In Bundibugyo, Dr Jonah is all but revered. As the pride of his people, he's a living example of what hope and resources mixed with talent and hard work can accomplish. Still, getting posted to Nyahuka was a struggle.

With his medical background, one might have expected that the Ministry of Health would have eagerly welcomed back this native son. After all, he is only the third doctor ever to come from Bundibugyo and the only one of the three who is currently caring for patients. One of the others is the top public health administrator for Bundibugyo and is no longer involved in direct patient care. The other was trained overseas, but now represents Bundibugyo in parliament. Two other Ugandan physicians work at the hospital but aren't from this district. They, along with Jonah, Scott and Jennifer, make up the five doctors who provide medical coverage for this district's 200,000 residents. With this ratio of 40,000:1, the healthcare needs are overwhelming, not surprisingly. Malaria is a major killer and Bundibugyo has one of the highest rates of sickle-cell disease in the world.

Despite these realities, assigning Jonah to work at Nyahuka took a miracle. The politics surrounding this were probably not unrelated to the fact that Jonah was from the 'wrong' ethnic group: a Mukonjo[1] in a district where power is centralised among the Babwisi. After months of delays, frustrating layers of bureaucracy, and numerous documents submitted and resubmitted, the chief administrative officer (CAO, pronounced 'cow'), a well-intentioned man who oversees all government appointments, agreed to make the assignment. Catching him on his last day in office before he was transferred to another district, Scott lobbied on Jonah's behalf. That CAO's final official act in Bundibugyo was to dictate and sign a letter confirming Jonah as the new head of Nyahuka Health Centre.

After the short five-minute ride, we reach the main gate and enter the compound. It's late in the afternoon at the end of the dry season, still too hot for anyone to be walking outside at this hour. On our way to the operating theatre, in the space where several ragged paths used to criss-cross a bowl of dust, we pass the beginnings of what will become a new maternity and paediatric building. Having modern, spacious wards for children and pregnant women, the two most frequent kinds of patients who come here, will usher this health centre into the twenty-first century. Scott and Jennifer's long-time dream of a new facility is in the early stages of becoming a reality, the result of funds from some generous benefactors. With the foundations laid, builders have begun to assemble the frame.

Jonah guides the motorcycle through the inner gate, past bed sheets hanging on the fence, and parks beside the garage-like building next to the lab which I've never been into. The charred remains of a fire smoulder nearby. In the shade of the veranda in front of the wards to our left, an elderly man is curled on a mat, sleeping. A young woman with short braids leans against the wall near him. Her eyes half-shut, she languidly watches a toddler crawling beside her.

Following Jonah into the building, my fingers tingle with expectation. We leave behind the stickiness of the air outside and step into a room that feels like a capsule designed to transport us to another world. The atmosphere is hushed with solemnity, and the reception area towards the back is empty except for a pair of black flip-flops. The walls are a sterile white, the ceilings unusually high. The burglar-proof windows, clamped shut and well above eye level, filter in hazy sunlight. The only sound I hear is the padding of our footsteps.

In the next room sits a silver industrial sink. Across from it, pastel green scrubs hang on hooks and two pairs of white wellington boots stand upright on the floor. Leaning over the sink, Jonah grabs a bar of soap and begins to scrub his hands and arms up to his elbows, repeating this action over and over.

'Pam, watch me and then do the same. Even though you're not part of the operation, you still need to glove and gown like us. After you scrub, put on everything.'

When he's finished, Jonah takes an outfit and disappears next door. I imitate his scrubbing, then throw a gown and apron over my dress and slide my feet into the oversize boots. My toes wiggle freely against the soft felt lining. I tie a hat over my hair and cover my mouth with a mask. Finally, I pull on a pair of latex gloves, the powder from them tickling my nose. As I look myself up and down draped in this strange attire, Jonah returns, gowned as I am.

'Can I take pictures?' Jonah glances at the small case holding my new camera and nods.

'Come, come let's go. We don't have much time.' I leave my bag hanging on a hook.

The theatre, which is the size of a modest New York City studio apartment, is uncluttered. Only a crash trolley and a low table line the wall on the left. Some empty shelves sit in the far corner, a portable screen pushed up beside them. The door at the far end of the room is a soft hue of pink. A midwife I recognise is already here along with two other women whom I take to be nurses. All dressed as we are, they look ready to begin.

In the centre of the room is a table lined with a white cloth and clear plastic sheet. A woman who looks less than thirty is lying on it in a foetal position, her eyes closed. Her bulging belly is covered with a brown tiger-printed *kitenge*. Beside her head is a tall pole holding a drip that's hooked up to the veins in her right hand.

As Jonah exchanges a few words with his team, the patient's eyes open and close. Jonah looks over the consent form the midwife has written out in the patient's blue exercise book, and hands it to me to read: *I Pierre consent for such an operation with anaesthesia as suggested by the surgeon/Dr for the best of my wife's health and the baby.* A thumb print is smudged on the top left corner.

'The patient herself doesn't have to give consent?' I ask.

'No, in a situation like this, it can be either the patient or her husband. They also want a tubal ligation, so I'll be able to show you that as well.'

'She's agreeing to have her tubes tied?'

Jonah confirms with the midwife. 'You discussed this with them?'

'Yes, Doctor, they have agreed to it.'

Jonah turns back to me. 'Sterilisation is not very common, but this is number six. Probably her husband can't feed any more children. They've come from Congo.'

Looking over the form again, I find myself wondering if the patient herself has in fact consented to be sterilised. There's no indication of that in her notebook. What's documented there is her husband's consent. When she wakes up in a few hours, will she learn she can no longer have children? Who will tell her? Or even worse, if she's not told now, will she become frustrated, and perhaps angry, when she realises in a year that her once fertile womb is no longer able to conceive? I hope she's been a part of this life-altering decision. But in her semi-conscious state, it's possible she hasn't. Seeing her lying there so helpless, so vulnerable, I have my doubts, but I don't think to probe further. I don't even think to ask what her name is, either.

This couple have come from across the border, six kilometres away, like 20 per cent of patients seen at Nyahuka each year. I assume this health centre must be closer than venturing to a similar facility in their own country. Crossing into Uganda at this point requires wading through a shallow river, the Semliki, or during the rainy season being carried above it by young, strong men, for a small fee. If you're Ugandan or

Congolese, the immigration authorities don't tend to ask for documents, making this type of travel uncomplicated.

'Are we ready?' Jonah asks his team. They nod. He gestures to one of the nurses.

'She's the anaesthetic nurse. The other one is a nursing assistant,' he tells me. 'We can't delay. The patient's been in labour already for over twenty-four hours.' The fatigue is evident on her face. As he talks, her eyes flicker again between shut and half-open. Beads of perspiration like soapsuds bubble across her forehead. The nurse nudges the woman onto her back and extends her hand. As she administers liquid in through the vein, the patient's eyes close for good. The nurse removes the *kitenge* and sets up a green sheet, creating a barrier between the patient's head and the rest of her body. She covers the woman with more green sheets, arranging them to create a triangle-shaped opening just below her belly button.

After sterilising this spot with an alcohol swab, Jonah takes a sharp blade and begins to make his incision. The skin parts and blood seeps out, in small droplets at first. I blink and gulp, squeezing my hands into tight balls, my fingernails cutting into my palms. I'm tempted to close my eyes, but I steady my gaze and will myself to keep watching. Jonah continues with a clean vertical cut, which exposes several inches of thick muscle hidden beneath the skin. Once the incision is deep enough, he begins to peel back the layers. The blood vessels that he's severed start to ooze. Jonah pins down the skin, clamping it with silver tongs.

He and his team work efficiently and methodically, as if engaged in a ritual together, with Jonah as the lead. As the operation proceeds, he calls out instrument names and the assistant hands them to him from a tray within arm's reach. I stand back and observe, taking a few photos, trying to be inconspicuous. This view inside the human body fascinates me. I marvel at how well protected the baby is in the womb. I'm also aware Jonah's working quickly, trying to get to this baby in time.

After more painstaking minutes of prising the mother's abdomen open with further clamping and stretching, Jonah exclaims, 'Ah-ha, here's the wall of the uterus.' As he perforates it, a foul-smelling liquid the colour of muddy water squirts out, soaking his apron and splashing up onto his face mask. He jumps back. I do too. Recovering, Jonah reaches into the woman's gaping womb. Locating the baby's head with the skill of a trained surgeon, he lifts out an almost white mucous-covered newborn. The baby is still, as if wrapped in clear plastic like a frozen chicken one would buy in a Kampala superstore. Jonah examines the baby while the midwife clamps the umbilical cord and cuts it. Then he hands the newborn to her.

'It's a girl,' he tells us.

There's no movement or sound from the baby. The midwife places her on a table by the far wall. She covers the baby with her mother's *kitenge* and checks for a heartbeat and pulse. I'm convinced the baby is dead, but she may be alive – just barely.

Using a suction ball, the midwife removes as much mucous as she can from the baby's nose and mouth. Once she clears the airways, she covers them and using a hand pump administers oxygen. Then she gives tiny chest compressions. Alternating back and forth between oxygen and compressions, she works on the newborn while I plead silently for her life. Inside, I'm yelling, 'God, please save her. Save this child. You are able.'

Meanwhile Jonah continues to attend to his patient. The baby may be out but his work isn't over. As I watch him extract the placenta and discard it in a slop bucket, I keep pleading without making a sound, praying that this precious baby girl will make it.

'OK, let me look for the fallopian tubes,' says Jonah, poking around inside the patient's uterus. As he does, I conjure up the two-dimensional pictures I've seen of them in biology textbooks. I glance at the midwife. She's still bending over the baby giving chest compressions. I look back at Jonah.

'I know they're here.' A few seconds pass. 'Ah here's the first one.' He extends a long, pale innocuous rubber band for me to see, unlike the image I have in my head.

'That's it? How did you know how to find it?'

'Ah,' he says, chuckling. 'They teach us these things in medical school. I've done so many of these by now, I can't even count.'

He snips the tube and sutures both ends. When he finds the other tube, he repeats the process. Then he begins to sew up his patient. Going through layer by layer of muscle and tissue, he reverses what he did an hour before. The midwife looks up and wipes her upper lip using her gloved hand. How long will she be able to keep forcing air into those tiny lungs? 'God, help this baby to breathe,' I say to myself. Just as Jonah is about to finish repairing the woman's lower abdomen, the baby lets out a tentative, barely audible cry.

We all cheer.

# 21
## The Call

On Tuesday, I go along to the maternity ward after lunch to see how the new baby is doing. They've called her Nightie. I don't know where she is since the wiry narrow beds aren't numbered. Weaving through them, I pass many pregnant women stretched out side by side. One is snoring softly. Another one is eating. The newborn I'm looking for is hidden in the folds of a *kitenge*, balanced on the lap of an older man who must be her father, one of his arms propping her up. In the other, he's holding a plastic spoon with milk up to Nightie's tiny lips. She's sucking on it in small, eager motions.

I smile, thrilled to see this, but when I turn to look at Nightie's mother, my grin fades. She seems worse than she did when I saw her on the operating table. She looks at me but can't hold open her eyes. Her skin is dull and sandy. Her pillow is damp. I wonder if she's been able to eat yet. Then I notice a pole beside the bed. Silent nutrition, antibiotics or both, are dripping through a line that disappears into a large vein on her left hand. That's why the baby's being spoon-fed. This mother can't nurse her baby. I don't know how long it takes to recover from major surgery like a C-section, but this mother is struggling.

I exchange greetings with Nightie's father, trying to convey hope. He looks up from feeding Nightie, but doesn't return my optimism. The hollows of his eyes signal worry. I watch him feed Nightie a few more spoons of milk, but don't stay long. I tell him I'll stop by tomorrow.

The next morning at the HIV clinic, the clinical officer doesn't turn up. After waiting for more than an hour, we learn he's out of the district at a 'training' which no one knew about. It's 10.30 and the waiting room is buzzing with anxious patients, wondering who will see them. I go to look for Jonah and find him making ward rounds.

'I'll come when I finish here. Separate those who have symptoms from those just coming for Septrin. I'll see the symptomatic ones.'

Masika makes an announcement and gets them organised into two groups. Then she begins to count out two weeks' worth of Septrin tablets, putting them into small clear plastic bags for those without symptoms. Septrin, also known as co-trimoxazole, is an antibiotic people living with HIV take every day to keep their infections in check. The Ugandan government recommends it for all patients who aren't on antiretroviral drugs (ARVs). Since Nyahuka often runs out, I try to supplement that supply, buying several large tubs whenever I'm in Kampala.

'Septrin is over,' Masika tells me ten minutes after she begins dividing it up into pill packets.

'It's completely finished? Already?' I look at the empty tub Masika is waving in front of me. 'I don't have any more at the house,' I tell her. 'I checked before I came this morning.'

'What about Kisembo?' she asks.

'Good idea. Let me see if he has any. Don't give any packets out yet. If I can't get more, we'll have to send patients home with only one week's worth.'

Jumping onto my bike, I hurry over to Kisembo's drug shop. Located less than a minute away and on the edge of the clothing market that springs up here on Saturdays, his storefront couldn't be more convenient.

I'm glad to find him there. A fortyish, round-faced man, with a receding hairline and an upbeat attitude, Kisembo is my informal but reliable clinician and pharmacist. Since I returned,

184

whenever I have sick kids at my door, I write Kisembo a note and send them with the note to see him. He treats them, usually it's for malaria, and runs up a tab. Every few weeks, I stop to settle my bill. Kisembo is pals with Jonah, a fellow Mukonjo, and seems well connected. He's often a great source of gossip too.

'Kisembo, do you sell Septrin in bulk?' I ask, looking around at the packets of pills displayed in open cupboards.

'Yes, please. I have it,' he says, taking down a large white tub from a shelf behind him.

'Great. Do you have another one? Don't think we'll need it today, but just in case. They brought only half a container from the pharmacy and these patients depend on it, you know?' He retrieves another tub.

'You want it?'

I nod, hoping to keep the exchange short. I need to get back. As if reading my mind, he adds, 'Don't worry about the money. Settle when you're ready.' He gives me a broad smile, exposing flawless teeth.

I rush back to the health centre. Jonah is just arriving at the clinic.

'Jonah, thanks so much for coming.'

'I had to come,' he says, the blood vessels in his eyes pronounced. He looks exhausted from a full morning. 'Haven't you separated the patients? Why are there still so many here?'

'Don't worry, most only need Septrin. I had to go to get more from Kisembo. Those are the ones waiting for you.' I point to a dozen patients lined up on the bench outside his office. The office, typical of those here, is furnished with a desk, two chairs and an exam table, but no sink and no antibacterial disinfectant. No gloves, either.

'Send the first one in,' says Jonah, managing a smile.

The line outside his office grows now that he's here. By the time Jonah gets through seeing them all, and we give out Septrin and return the charts to the back office, I'm wiped out. I'm tempted to go straight home, but I said I'd go and see Nightie's mother. I decide to check with Jonah first.

'How's Nightie's mother?'

'No improvement,' he says, his tone heavy. I can't tell if that's because he's tired, or she's not doing well, or both. I nip over to the ward for a quick visit. Nightie's father is keeping watch at his wife's bedside, anxiety etched across his forehead. Nightie is asleep on a mat in the shadow of the bedframe. Her mother, still non-responsive, looks much the same. I don't stay long.

That night, Nightie's mother dies.

When I hear this from Jennifer the next day, I can't believe it. She's dead? It's as if I've just had the wind knocked out of me. When I saw Nightie's mother the day before, she hadn't improved, but I assumed she was stable. She was feeble, yes, but I expected her to recover. I had no idea that she wouldn't make it. None whatsoever. She wasn't technically my patient, but I've never known anyone, whose care I felt invested in, die within days of watching them get life-saving medical attention.

That evening after dinner, I seek out the safety of my own company to look at the photos I took in the operating theatre. Now I feel like a trespasser who invaded this woman's last few precious days on this earth. Did *I* bother to get her consent for these images? Would I feel differently had I done so? And if she'd granted it, would I have still taken these if I'd known a week later, she'd no longer be alive? I try to grasp for answers, but they don't come.

Wondering how Jonah's coping with her death, I make a point of looking for him the next time I'm at Nyahuka. When I enter the compound that Saturday afternoon, another steamy day, I see him outside the ward, standing in the shade of the veranda.

'Jonah, how are things?'

'Not bad.'

'I wanted to thank you for helping out on Wednesday.'

'Those patients needed to be seen. Some of them are quite ill, you know.'

'True.' I pause. 'Jonah, can I ask you something?'

'Of course.'

'What happened to our patient?'

'The baby seems to be doing OK, but the mother, she didn't pull through.' His voice is calm, unaffected, even.

'It's so sad. Were you surprised?' I try to hold my voice steady. I get distressed just thinking about her.

'I wasn't surprised.' Jonah's unemotional. It disarms me.

'Really? Why not?'

'You remember during the surgery, when that brown liquid splashed all over me? That's not normal. That smell was the sign of a major infection in the uterus. Of course, I didn't know about it until I was inside her.'

I grimace, recalling that horrible stench. It smelled like an undrained sewer, but it happened so fast when Jonah was trying to get to Nightie, I didn't dwell on it. Not wanting to think too much about her mother yet, I focus on Nightie.

'I'm glad the baby made it.'

'The family is very fortunate,' Jonah tells me. 'If the baby had been in there much longer, she wouldn't have been alive by the time I reached her. Of course, now that her mother is gone, it's going to be very difficult since she won't be getting breast milk. The father will have to try to find a woman in the family to care for the baby. Perhaps his sister.'

His words take me back to my first day here at the health centre two years ago, to that grandmother who was nursing her malnourished granddaughter. How amazing that that is sometimes possible. I pray Nightie will be as fortunate as that child was. She's already proved that she's a survivor. I try to picture her nursing at the breast of one of her aunties.

'I think she'll be OK,' I say, more hopeful than I feel. Then, I press Jonah for more. 'Jonah, after going through with that C-section which saved the baby, aren't you terribly disappointed to lose her mother? I'm still working through in my own mind how it happened. I never expected her to die.'

'Look,' he says, dabbing his face with a cloth he retrieves from his pocket, 'this is the reality of practising medicine, especially here. Many terrible things take place that wouldn't happen if we had more resources to do our best for the patients. If they had come sooner, before the mother's labour was very advanced, she might have had a different outcome.' He goes on, 'Deaths like this happen in Bundibugyo almost every day. Not from a C-section, but mothers who die from obstructed labour, especially at home, it's very common. This was different because we were able to save the baby. It just wasn't possible to save the mother.'

I wait a moment and then can't resist asking him: 'Jonah, how do you live with this, with these kinds of deaths, if they happen so often?'

'Medicine is like this. It has risks. We know that when we go into this profession. We do our best with what we have, but sometimes it's not good enough. We have to accept that.' He dabs his brow again. 'Death is part of life, whether you work in medicine or not.'

'But it seems to strike so much here.'

Jonah nods, adding, 'Yes, death can sometimes come very quickly.' He looks away towards the outline of the Rwenzoris, smoky and purple in the distance. Then he lowers his voice and looks at me again. 'Bundibugyo is a very difficult place to practise medicine. Extremely difficult at times. If I didn't have a deep sense that this was my calling, that this is where God wants me to be, I wouldn't be here. I wouldn't be able to do this day after day.'

After a moment, he heads back into the ward. I stand there pondering his honesty, grateful for his deep sense of commitment and relieved that, like me on the really hard days, it's his sense of calling that enables him to stick this out. Jonah has become such an essential presence in Bundibugyo, I hope he stays here for a long, long time.

# 22
# The Celebration

The paediatric and maternity building beckons, glossy white with a turquoise strip demarcating the height of the wrap-around veranda. On this sun-drenched afternoon, this structure, erected over the last three months, resembles a pearl brooch encircled by malachite and diamonds. Where tufts of grass and several well-worn paths had once been, now stands an impressive twenty-first century facility, transforming the beleaguered health centre into a small hospital. Scott and Jennifer raised the funds through foreign donors, but the vision is to turn this building over to the Ministry of Health now that it's finished.

We've come down as a team to tour the facility for the first time and to thank God for this gift. I tiptoe in after the others and, like them, slip off my sandals, not wanting to soil the sparkling new eggshell-white tiles. We wander through the spacious ward, its walls matching the tiles. It houses forty beds with mattresses arranged in five alcoves of eight clusters. We exclaim at their child-friendly colours of red, yellow and blue. It's thrilling to imagine all the good that will unfold here in the coming years. Scott leads us in a time of prayer for the many children who'll regain their health in this place, before our large group starts to shuffle next door.

I hang back even though the fresh paint is causing me to wince. I marvel at the contrast between the spotlessness of this space and the former grimy one for kids at the back of the compound. There, mothers and fathers and grandparents sleep cramped in single beds, huddled next to their babies and toddlers on mattresses they've brought from home. When that ward reaches capacity, families sprawl out on banana fibre mats which offer meagre comfort from the hard floor. Hearing an 'Amen' brings me back to the new building. I hurriedly follow the rest of the team into the maternity ward.

This large area is twice the size of the current poky one. With a dozen beds and an airy delivery room, the high ceiling and windows invite light but ensure privacy. I join the others who're already praying for all the women whose babies will enter the world here, hopeful that many more mums will opt to give birth here than at home. As we file out, again I linger, savouring the sacredness of this space. This pristine building will stay unfilled for only a few more short hours. Tomorrow, we will give away this family jewel. Then the sick, the dying and the expectant will all come here seeking restored health, renewed strength and new life.

During breakfast the next day, there's a knock at the door. It's Jonah.

'The tie looks good,' I say, giving him a thumbs up.

'This is a big day for us, you know,' he chuckles. His eyes are sparkling. 'I came to ask if you could type this for me.' He hands me two handwritten pages.

'No problem. Please come in. Have some tea with Pat. She just got back last week.' While I work on his speech, Jonah takes a seat at the dining table with Pat and Sonja, a friend of mine visiting from New York.

Later, after he leaves, the three of us walk over to Scott and Jennifer's. It's dry and cloudless, perfect for an outdoor event. We're assembling at their home to greet today's guest of honour, the new American ambassador, but I'm not quite sure what to expect. The closest I've come to this was when the previous ambassador flew in to acknowledge the high HIV testing rates occurring due to the success of Kwejuna. This occasion is on a far grander scale. This building will impact this area for years, perhaps decades to come. Hence, a community-wide celebration and a distinguished public servant to conduct the handover to the Ugandan government seem fitting.

When we arrive, the ambassador is already there. Tall, bald and with a full greying beard, he resembles a slender Santa Claus who's shed the red and white suit for a navy blazer and a pair of tan slacks. The living room is at capacity with the whole team present, making the space seem warmer than it is. Perhaps I'm also noticing the temperature because I'm wearing a blue and white knee-length top and matching trousers that I bought in Fort Portal.

'Call me by my first name,' he says when he begins, 'because as my wife frequently reminds me, the stature goes with the title and not with the person.' His humility is genuine. He flew in that morning, not on the US-government-issued jet for America's top representative in Uganda, but on a six-seater plane, a bit bigger than the one I arrived in almost three years ago. His only companion on the flight was the Member of Parliament for women in Bundibugyo.

Scott has put together a montage of photos highlighting our various programmes.

'We have five PhDs so we're an overeducated team,' Scott says, stating the obvious, and not mentioning that because he and Jennifer are physicians, that puts us at a total of seven doctors. This concentration of talent is unusual, I suspect, for missionaries in such a remote place.

'Amazing,' the ambassador responds, a wide smile forming. 'Thank you so much for being here. The work you're doing in this area of the country is really impressive but more importantly, it's so necessary. How long has your mission been here?'

'Since the eighties,' Scott tells him. 'The work began with starting churches and Bible translation. Community development came later.'

'The United States gives 500 million dollars to the Ugandan government every year,' he tells us, 'but America's greatest asset is its people. What you're all doing here, this hospital, the water project, the school, is exactly that. You should be proud. Very proud.' He scans the room, smiling. I'm not American, by ethnicity or by nationality, but since America has become my adopted home, I'll pass as an honorary citizen, at least for today.

The compound at Nyahuka has become the scene of an outdoor fête. The new building is decorated with blue, pink and white balloons tied to the front veranda and there's a huge awning erected for spectators. A special tent for the guests of honour, decorated with pink and orange balloons, is across from it. Several red velvet couches, lined up as if for a recording of a chat show, are at the front. Besides the ambassador, the women's MP, and the new CAO, other dignitaries are expected as well.

Adjacent to this tent are three more awnings overhanging rows and rows of plastic chairs. The health workers are sitting on one side, and almost everyone is dressed in rarely seen lab coats, bleached a gleaming white. Many have a yellow patch with the mother and child Kwejuna logo sewn onto their sleeves. On the other side sit community members in their Sunday best. Most women have styled their hair. Men are decked out in crisp ironed shirts.

The atmosphere is charged with anticipation. Popular songs, some of them in Swahili, though it's not spoken here, ring out over a public address system. The young daughter of one of the nurses' aides wanders through the rows in a party dress dotted with pink roses, hoisting a bottle of water like a new toy. The gurgling of her laughter is heard between songs. People from Nyahuka Town who weren't invited press against the fence, determined to join in.

Sonja, Pat and I make our way to the health workers' tent. Scott and Jennifer are with the VIPs. As we take our seats, Masika, whose hair is shaped into a maroon-dyed bob, pokes me in the back. When I turn around, she has a broad smirk on her face.

'Pam.Ella, you look so smart.' She's pointing at my trousers and nodding.

'They look OK?'

'Very smart.'

I grin back. Though I'm breaking the rules, I've managed not to offend.

When the guests are seated, the speeches begin. Jonah is one of the first speakers. Wearing a white coat I've not seen before, with his name, 'Jonah Kule, MD', embroidered across his chest on the left in red letters, he looks like a medical director from Mulago, Uganda's largest hospital in Kampala. He opens by thanking the mission and the American people for the gift of the new building. Then he gets straight to the heart of his message.

'Nyahuka receives one-twentieth of the money that Bundibugyo Hospital gets, but we treat three-quarters of the patients seen at the hospital. We therefore request consideration in increasing funding to this health centre.' There is murmuring from the crowd. 'Regarding staffing, we lack clinical officers, midwives, anaesthetists and doctors. For doctors, it is a general problem in the country, but worse in Bundibugyo. There is no incentive to attract doctors to come here from outside the district.'

I scan the audience. While there's no reaction from the front row of dignitaries, their faces veiled behind sunglasses, lips firm and unchanging, healthcare workers near us begin to nod and mumble, agreeing with Jonah.

Buoyed by their support, Jonah gets personal. 'It takes more than just being born here to accept work here because even though the Bundibugyo doctor is paid the same as one in well-endowed districts, the amount of work we are doing is far greater because we are so few. A doctor in Bundibugyo earns the same salary as a doctor in Kampala, but the Kampala doctor works much less hours per week, having time to do other work to increase his income, but a doctor in this district works up to seven days. I would appeal to the district leaders to take this matter seriously as we could come to a time when there is almost no doctor in the district.'

This situation can't be overstated. Working in Bundibugyo is a hardship post, and that's not just because of the tremendous workload. Besides the lack of plumbing and the dearth of trained staff or adequate supplies, Bundibugyo is riddled with an ineffective bureaucracy and a lack of fiscal accountability. An initial sense of service or even curiosity might motivate you to come here in the first place. But to commit to investing in this community long-term means you're either crazy, exceptional, or have a deep sense of calling.

Jonah ends with: 'Thank you. For God and for my country.' The compound at Nyahuka explodes with cheers and shouts, some standing to applaud him. Although he could have taken a plum job in Kampala, he's come back, putting his people before his own ambitions. With his two oldest daughters away at boarding school, he's also made difficult personal choices.

My heart swells with admiration. Leaders like Jonah give me hope for Uganda, and for Africa as a whole. The truth is, though, there aren't enough like him. How I wish we had more, a whole generation, even, willing to sacrifice for the greater good. So many people who I grew up with in Nigeria have settled in the UK, or the US, or Canada. Of course, I'm no different.

And yet, going back home to settle is complicated. Abroad, we've become accustomed to a more efficient and comfortable way of life, one that rewards hard work and means greater opportunities for our children. Then there are the obligations of caring for extended family members. Sometimes these responsibilities can seem 'easier' to manage from a distance, especially when they are offset by funds which are sent home regularly. Many of us living overseas provide this type of support. Then, if you've been away and you return home, you're expected to help – financially and in other ways – those who haven't had the same opportunities as you. This can be daunting, and so many of us opt not to take up these expectations. Jonah seems to be a rare exception.

Once he sits down, adolescent girls in maroon dresses follow, singing, dancing and swaying. As they twirl around forming a large circle, sweat trickles off their faces and stains form around their armpits. An elaborate skit, designed to encourage women to come to this new facility to deliver their babies instead of having them at home, follows the dancing. They hoist a woman onto a stretcher, her belly enlarged with padding, and act out bringing her to Nyahuka. Relatives follow, carrying a mat and bed sheets. We all laugh. Mattresses might now be here but family members will still have to bring everything else a patient will need for a stay in this new hospital.

We listen to more speeches. They share a common theme: thanking the mission for its generosity, not just for the building but for its many years of service to this community. Ugandans are a grateful people, quick to say 'thank you', and that is on full display. In response, Scott acknowledges the appreciation, but reminds us more than once that all we have comes from God.

When the speeches are over, Scott and Jennifer escort the ambassador over to the paediatric ward for the ribbon cutting. Jonah and the VIP entourage follow. I sneak out of my chair to watch, concealed beside the photographer. Scott rips off the brown paper, unveiling two plaques on the wall beside the ribbon. The one on the left thanks those who have donated funds to make the building possible. The other, flanked with small American and Ugandan flags, declares that the ambassador has opened the building. Scott hands the ambassador a pair of scissors. The ambassador cuts the blue ribbon with a quick snip and drops the keys into Jonah's palms. The crowd cheers and claps.

When Jonah unlocks the door, the crowd erupts again, louder this time. As the VIPs step inside, I head back to my seat. We continue applauding and yelling until they exit the building. Then, just before they reach their seats, Scott, wearing a tie and blue blazer, maybe for the first time ever here, raises both hands in the air and dances a jig. The crowd explodes into howls of laughter, music blares out of the speakers, and the real celebrating begins.

We mill around, talking, laughing, greeting old friends, taking photos and reliving the remarkable occasion we've just witnessed: a building conceived and constructed for the express purpose of letting it go. And in giving it away, many will be blessed for years to come. For this single glorious afternoon, all the injustices heaped on this embattled place are set aside: the poverty and pain, the sadness and sorrow, the inefficiencies and inadequacies, the lives snatched away too early in death, and even Jesika lying in a bed nearby in the women's ward. Those things are all secondary right now. Instead, on this joyful occasion, revelling in this party and celebrating this gift – this gleaming pearl which is of such 'great value'[1] – is like experiencing a foretaste of heaven.

All I want to do is soak in the fun and goodwill, and preserve the feelings of gratitude and happiness and celebration that are mingling together in a delightful crescendo. I'd like to feast on the community meal that will follow too, but I can't hang around. Sonja has a plane to catch. She's flying out with the ambassador, so we say our goodbyes and leave just as the party is starting. As we walk back up to the duplex to collect her bags, dust kicking up under our shoes, the boom-boom-boom of the music follows us until we are well past the market.

The next morning, we hear that the first woman to deliver in the new maternity ward is a Kwejuna mother. Giving birth last night hours after the festivities ended, she's named her son Scott, but in true Babwisi style, he'll be known as Scottie.

# 23
# The Mystery

I'm on my way to Nyahuka to visit Jesika. When Pat returned at the end of June, without hesitating she set in motion the process for transferring Jesika from the hospital to the health centre. This way Jonah can be involved, Jesika's mother can help to care for her, and her daughters can come and visit often too. Since the community party, Pat has begun to spend all her spare moments with Jesika. She takes food over in the mornings, brings back barely eaten dishes in the evenings, and repeats the same routine all over again the next day. Last night at dinner, Pat told me why Jesika's not eating.

'Jonah's diagnosed Jesika as stage four. She's on a drip.'

'That's not a good sign,' I said, stating the obvious.

Absently swirling her near-empty wine glass, Pat continued as if she hadn't heard me. 'Her throat's covered in ulcers. She's got thrush. Wish she could get on ARVs.' Her voice had tapered off. 'But Jonah says it's too late. She wouldn't be able to get them down.'

Hearing this, I'd wondered: could Jesika be nearing the end? I didn't ask Pat. Instead, I decided to go to find out for myself.

When I enter the compound the following morning, seeing the gleaming paediatric and maternity building, open now for almost a month, makes me smile. Recalling what a fantastic celebration we'd had, I wave at the pregnant woman sitting on the veranda outside the maternity ward, delighted that she's come here to give birth. Continuing past it, I walk behind the lab and head through the second set of gates to the old adult wards.

I find Jesika in a small room off the main hallway of the women's unit. The walls are grubby, and privacy is fleeting. A *kitenge*, crudely tied across metal bars on the window, provides only partial cover from prying eyes that might peer in from outside. Sprawled on a wrinkled sheet covering a worn mattress pushed into a corner, Jesika looks up at me from beneath heavy lids, but her eyes soon close. A plate of plantains, which look cold, is on the floor next to her, a blue thermos and several plastic cups beside it. A bottle of fluid hanging from a nail driven into the wall above her connects a tube to her right hand.

There's no sign of Pat, but squeezed beside Jesika on the mattress are her mother and Ester, a friend of Jesika's, who has creamy brown skin and broad hips. Another woman I don't know is seated at the other end, near Jesika's ankles. Jesika's husband is no longer around. I wonder if he disappeared as quickly as he turned up.

Her mother, with eyes swollen and her jaw tight, beckons me to sit. Removing my slippers, I squat down by the door. Then, noticing Jesika's bare legs, I lean in. My fingers pull the *kitenge* across her, grazing her limbs. They're on fire, causing me to flinch. Seeing Jesika like this, I don't know what to say, and this time I'm grateful for the language barrier. We sit for some moments in silence, listening to her laboured breathing. She wheezes as if in pain. Then I remember. I do know some Lubwisi.

'Can we sing something?' I ask. Her mother nods. I begin with the first line of the chorus of a familiar hymn we often sing in church.

> *Kangumire Hali Jesu*
> Let me cling to Jesus[1]

My voice quivers because I'm nervous and my mouth is dry, but I press on. Soon, the others join me.

> *Kan-gu-mi-re Ha-li Je-su*
> Let me cling to Jesus
> *Byona Ebyensi Butarumu*
> Everything of the world is worthless
> *Byona Ebyen-si Bu-ta-mu-ru*
> Everything of the world is worthless

I repeat the chorus again and the others follow with the verses. Not knowing those words, I hum along, straining. Our combined voices aren't strong, and we're grieving, but for a few tender moments the gentle melody slices through the thickness, as if reducing the distance between earth and heaven. Jesika's eyes remain closed, her body unmoving. When we finish, repeating the chorus several more times, the woman I don't know begins singing another hymn I recognise. Not sure of those words, I hum along. Then she leads us in another. We repeat this over and over with me humming along when I can. The four of us join together to bring comfort to ailing Jesika. Or maybe this spontaneous choir is more for our aching hearts than it is for her.

When our singing winds down, I don't hang around. I stagger out of Jesika's room onto the veranda. Shaken at how close to death Jesika seems and how near it has now come to me, I look down at my hands. They're trembling.

Pat took Jesika home from the health centre yesterday. It was against Jonah's advice, but Pat knew Jesika's end was coming and she wanted to give her daughters a final chance to see their mother alive in their own home. A sign that she was ready to let go, Jesika had begun yanking out the needle piercing her hand.

This situation with Jesika hasn't done much for my sleep. Plus, August has come and we have some visitors here from the US. I really enjoy being with them, but it's meant lingering more than usual over meals, and long full evenings together. While

Pat was making the arrangements to bring Jesika home, I took our American friends to the Congo border. It was fascinating to watch strong young men hoisting women, babies and goods on their shoulders and hauling them across the Semliki River. Several immigration officials were relaxing under nearby mango trees. I was tempted to try crossing the border, in the opposite direction, but suspect the men in blue uniforms would've demanded our passports, which we hadn't brought.

Now, it's Wednesday morning and though still drowsy after a cold shower, I'm making my way to our midweek prayer meeting at Scott and Jennifer's, which begins at 6.30. Pat didn't come back to the duplex last night and I haven't heard from her. Strange. No text, no call.

I soon learn why.

'We heard the first wails after midnight,' JD tells us, her voice sounding like she has a head cold. 'They woke me and Kevin up. I knew they must be coming from Jesika's, across the fence. They got louder and louder through the night. I guess once people realised, they wanted to be there with her mother and the girls.'

When I hear this at first, I'm dazed, unable to sort through my feelings. Jesika's death became inevitable but now that I know she's gone, I don't feel the relief I thought I might. I assumed Jesika's passing would release some of the angst I've felt due to her rapid demise, but it hasn't. At least not yet. Not in these early moments. I feel dismayed and confused.

I'm not able to focus during our ninety minutes together, and find myself unable to tune in to those who we're praying for. After we wrap up, all of us women walk down to Jesika's. Wailing and screaming meet us on the main road even before we turn down the path towards her house. When we get there, I realise the cries are coming from the room where her body lies. We sit on benches assembled topsy-turvy in the small yard, watching and waiting our turn for a few moments with the corpse.

I look for the children, my mind hazy. I don't see Jesika's daughters, but after some time, I notice their cousin, a ten-year-old who lives with them. An inconspicuous bystander in his own home, he's standing alone away from the benches, leaning against a tree and looking around. I wonder if this is the largest group he's ever seen gathered in this space. I fixate on him until he finds my stare. His sockets are hollow, his eyes glazed over, his customary cheekiness absent. I try to meet his gaze with sympathy and kindness, but hardly know what I'm feeling, and I'm not sure how to convey emotions which are foreign to me. In the few seconds we connect, I see nothing but emptiness in the darks of his eyes. When he turns his face away, I can't help but wonder how this heart-rending loss of his aunt, occurring within his own home, will impact his young life.

When it's my turn to go inside, I squint to adjust to the dimness of the small room, crowded with bodies. The space has an oppressive, stale odour. Is this what death smells like? I make out the silhouettes of other women, distinguishable by their headscarves. In the far corner, I pick out Jesika's body laid out on a narrow mattress. Covered up to her neck in a light-coloured sheet, she looks more at peace than I've seen her during my recent hospital visits. The loud sobbing I first heard has subsided, replaced by a whimpering, like a puppy in distress. Jesika's mother, who's lying on a mat beside her, remains tearful and drawn. A usually cheerful teenage friend of Jesika's is present but solemn. A distraught Ester, who was in the hospital room, is there too, moaning, limp and defeated. I sit with them, remaining still, hesitant to exhibit signs of life among the mourning.

As I grieve with Jesika's friends, I speculate about what they'll learn from her premature death. Will they go to get tested for HIV at the health centre, where free tests are offered three days a week and results are ready in half an hour? And if they learn they're living with HIV, will they seek out the drugs which can extend their lives? Or will they too succumb to the shame that appears to have paralysed Jesika, trapping her like a prisoner in her own body, unable to grant her permission to acknowledge her condition and seek help?

I have no idea how they'll respond, but I only hope her pain-filled struggle to face the reality of AIDS will be redemptive, though right now, it's hard to see what that would look like. As I take in this wretched scene, my own anger festers. There's a simmering of emotions threatening to erupt. Jesika's passive response to her diagnosis makes me want to lash out. But how and to whom? It's as if she's slapped me in the face and immobilised my hands so I can't fight back. My cheeks sting, as if red and raw, making the tragedy of her situation and the pain she's inadvertently inflicted resound even more.

Contemplating Jesika's tragic journey with HIV, I'm tempted to conclude that no matter how much we care, however much we give of ourselves here hoping to have an impact, our work feels inadequate and insufficient. Despite our best efforts, death and loss persist. Yet I also have to cling to the bigger reality that death doesn't have the final say. I honestly believe that. At the same time, Jesika's death at this young age – was she even thirty yet? – seems so unnecessary.

That afternoon, hoping for some closure, I join others to support the family as they bury Jesika deep in the forest on land her mother owns. When the pallbearers pour in sand to fill the cavity where they've just laid Jesika's coffin, Ester collapses at the graveside. She flails around on the ground, screaming as if having an epileptic seizure. When it gets almost unbearable, her anguished cries tormenting the crowd, two men approach. As she writhes and struggles to resist them, they lift her up and carry her away.

# Part Three

Part Three

# 24
# The Disease

Following Jesika's death, Pat and I took time away at the resort on the edge of Lake Victoria to grieve and recover. The respite was so helpful. The answers to my questions about 'why' remain elusive and I still abhor the ignominy of AIDS, but I return to Bundibugyo determined to throw myself back into the Kwejuna Project. Before I know it, November arrives, signalling that I've only got about six weeks left here.

At the end of that first week, one afternoon as I stare at the screen waiting for my email to download, I hear a *boda boda* pull up to the duplex. When the engine outside goes silent, I pull myself away and head to the front door. Through the mesh screen, I see Jonah walking towards me. He eases a helmet off his head, his face shiny and damp. A slim man I don't recognise, wearing a mechanic's navy jumpsuit, stays behind with the motorcycle.

'Hello, Pam,' Jonah says, his expression sombre.

'Jonah, welcome,' I say, holding open the door. 'Please come inside.'

'No, we can't come in now. Listen, can I ask you to type something while we wait? We need to have this report as soon as possible.'

'Of course.'

Together, we go over the three pages which describe his visit earlier that day to Kikyo. The new CAO asked him to investigate the mysterious deaths that are affecting his ethnic group, the Bakonjo. This must be the same disease Kisembo told me about. From the symptoms patients reported – high fever, diarrhoea, vomiting and abdominal pain – Jonah thinks it's probably typhoid.

They visited a home in Bugharama, where Jonah examined two patients. Three in that house had already died. Then they made their way to Kikyo Health Centre, where Jonah saw seven more patients. Those people seem to be recovering. They're taking quinine for malaria and two types of antibiotics: Cipro and Septrin. The patients must've bought these themselves because Jonah notes there were no drugs in the entire facility. His report asks for basic medicines and he appeals to the Ministry of Health and World Health Organization for help in confirming the disease.

Jonah also held a meeting with the staff and other community members there. He stressed handwashing after caring for patients and boiled water for drinking, neither of which is routinely done here. As the only Bakonjo physician in this district, Jonah's in a unique position to counter the widespread fear of witchcraft through poisoning. He's not only one of them but because of his medical training and the respect he commands, he, more than anyone else, can convince them that what they're dealing with is a disease that has a biomedical explanation. It's not the result of evil spirits. Reading about Jonah's efforts to restore confidence among his people, I can't help but think God's placed him in this unique position 'for such a time as this'.[1]

While Jonah and his colleague wait in the shade outside, I speed through the report, print two copies and rush them out to him. As he mounts the back of the motorcycle, I remind him about next week.

'Jonah, see you and Mellen and the girls on Tuesday?'

'Don't worry, we'll be there.'

'Come any time after 6.30.'

The motorcycle makes its way down the driveway dodging mud puddles and turns right, back towards Bundibugyo Town.

I had my first goodbye this morning, before the rain came. Late afternoon drops are pelting down on the zinc roof, causing a drumming sound to reverberate throughout the duplex. The force of a storm like this usually scares me, making me worried about discovering a leak somewhere. But right now, I'm not bothered, cocooned in the safety of my bedroom. Lying on my bed, gazing up at the ceiling, which I notice could do with a fresh coat of paint, I'm savouring the memory of the TBA programme this morning, relieved this downpour held off until it was all over. The aprons turned out really well. Though Rose had charged me more and used more material than Agnes – which means I'm left with an extra roll of material – after I got over being annoyed with her, I had to conclude that she was the better businesswoman. The TBAs loved the aprons and packed the community centre, filling it with loud clapping when I held the first one up to show it to them. What they didn't realise at first was that the aprons were also a parting gift.

I stuttered when I told them this would be our last gathering. Some women gasped when Masika conveyed the message; others shook their heads in disbelief. Watching their faces, I had a hard time getting the words out. I acknowledged the TBAs for delivering so many babies all over the district, thanked them for their eagerness to learn, and affirmed their willingness to be part of the effort to prevent HIV in Bundibugyo.

In those moments, I regretted I hadn't made my exit date known months before, during my regional trainings with them. At the time, I thought telling them so far in advance would make them question my commitment and translate into awkwardness between us. I was already feeling conflicted that I'd not been able to give them as much time as I had when I first came to Bundibugyo. Yet now, since my announcement has taken them so much by surprise, I see that I have disappointed and maybe even hurt some of them.

As they absorbed the news, one of the TBA leaders stood up.

'Miss Pam.Ella. We very sad you going. If we know, if you tell us, we give you pa-tee.'

'*Weebale*, thank you for thinking of a party. I'm so sorry I didn't tell you before today.'

As each one came up to receive her apron, we hugged. Many enthused, '*Weebale mono*,' thanking me over and over. Some also said, 'God bless you.' From others, it was: 'May God add more.' With one of my favourite women, I thanked her for giving me a live chicken when Masika and I visited her home in Bundibugyo Town, and we clung together for a long moment. When the oldest woman there, probably in her seventies, with her cheeky smile and silver hair, grabbed me, a tear threatened to push its way out of my eye.

Then, without me saying anything, as each one received her apron, she slipped it over her clothes. When they were all in uniform, I took a final photo. They resembled a gospel choir robed in royal blue ready for worship. Afterwards, we went outside to enjoy our last meal together. During lunch, as we laughed and reminisced, I forgot my sadness. Filling up with rice and beans and *matoke*, I savoured the company of these courageous yet marginalised women toiling in this end-of-the-road place, so grateful to have worked with them. Once we were full, as at other TBA gatherings, many whipped out plastic bags, stuffing leftovers into them for another meal with their children and husbands at home.

By this time, the event was all but over, but they hung around. Then, taking me by the hand and leading me back into the community centre, they encircled me and began dancing, singing first in Lubwisi, and then in Lukonjo. Interwoven with songs, they thanked me over and over again for working with them, for my support and interest in their role, and for the aprons. Resisting the urge to disappear from all this attention, I managed a big smile and danced along, which drew even more cheers and laughter. Finally, as if this spontaneous party wasn't enough of a sign of their gratitude, one of the women whipped off her headscarf, fashioned it into a cap, and solicited donations. On the spot, these indigent women – many old enough to be my mother, others reminding me of the Fulani grandmother I was named after but never knew – reached into their bras and pockets, and from hidden places threw in coins and notes. Half an hour later, when the singing and collecting were over, they had contributed almost USh20,000 (£5)! Embarrassed at this effusive and unexpected display of gratitude, I was unable to speak, but that didn't matter. They gave specific instructions. The funds were for me to buy material to have an outfit made. Whenever I wore it, I was to remember them.

Now hours after that fantastic send-off, the affection and generosity of those women has left me radiating with warmth and appreciation, full and expansive. Their celebration of me was so, so undeserved, and the afterglow is sweet. Listening to walls of water slap the outside of the bedroom, I keep replaying the day's events in my mind. As I try to embed these memories in a place where I will savour them for a long time, I can't help but recall what these faithful farmers believe: rain is a sign of God's pleasure.

As evening approaches, the downpour subsides, giving way to the after-rain smell of freshness. I'm glad the weather has settled down. Pat and I have been trying to remain patient, waiting for Jonah and his family to join us for dinner. Even more than Masika, and perhaps linked to our shared interest in healthcare, I feel closer to him than any other Ugandan, so I've made sharing a meal with him a priority before I leave.

Long after the day has ended, when night creatures are chirping and jasmine from the bush in front perfumes the air, we hear a vehicle pull into the driveway. I rush to the door and, pushing open the screen, I see Jonah and Mellen tumbling out of their van with their two youngest daughters.

'Welcome, welcome everyone. So glad you made it.'

They come through into the living-dining room and sink into a couch.

'Pam, sorry we've come so late.'

'Jonah, no problem. Please, please everyone, sit at the table,' I urge. 'The food is ready.'

'Would the girls like a mat?' Pat asks as they move over to the table. Mellen looks down at her three-year-old, wearing a red sweater over her blue uniform and clinging to her thigh.

'Don't worry about it, Pat. Let them sit at the table. The small one will sit with me.'

'It's been a long day,' Jonah explains. 'After the clinic this morning, I went to Bundibugyo Town. Then, when the rain finished, we had to go to Kirindi. Make sure there was no problem with our house from the rain.'

'I hope everything was OK?' I ask.

Jonah nods.

'How was the road?' Pat asks.

'So bad, especially coming back in the dark. The van was sliding. I had to drive very carefully.' I picture their van floating on a sea of mud, their heads bobbing from side to side. Jonah is one of the few people who can afford a vehicle here. He only drives it in the district and never in Kampala, so the police won't discover he doesn't have a licence.

We pile our plates with rice, beans and Nigerian stew, steam rising. Shying away from politics, the hardship of life in Bundibugyo, and the still unconfirmed mystery disease, we laugh a lot. Jonah tells the story of how he met Mellen, who was a shy student. She keeps revising what he says. Their marriage has lasted more than fifteen years, a lifetime in this area. They're a good fit: he with a flamboyant, gregarious personality, she a quiet but solid and capable partner. They are raising five daughters together and Mellen is pregnant with their sixth child.

After dinner, we move over to the sofas and drink cups of sweet, milky tea. By this time, the little one is asleep in her mother's arms, a bubble of spit collecting in the corner of her mouth. Her sister, also dressed in her school uniform the colour of the TBA aprons, with a pink sweater on top, is nodding off beside her father. Her head leans into the crook of his armpit, and every now and then, she wakes herself up. After one of these head jerks, Mellen notices.

'We should be going. The children are tired. They have school tomorrow.' She looks at Jonah.

'It's true,' Jonah agrees. 'Pam, thank you for cooking. Pat, thank you too.' He stretches out his legs and stands.

'Thank *you*,' I say. 'I'm sorry I haven't invited you for dinner before now. I wanted to do it at least once before I go.'

'When are you leaving?'

'Middle of December.'

'So, we still have a few weeks with you.'

'The time will go fast.'

He nods. 'That's how life is.'

'Jonah, will you be at the clinic tomorrow?'

'Am off duty.'

I grab a lamp as Pat and I follow Jonah and Mellen outside. Each parent hauls a sleeping child slung over their shoulder like a sack of cassava back to the van. Jonah turns the headlights on and after a false start, when he tries the ignition a second time, the engine comes alive. He reverses, steers the vehicle around the mango tree and heads towards the road. Pat and I wave, watching until the darkness swallows them up.

# 25
# The Outbreak

I've begun counting the days. Not because I'm eager to leave, but so I can cram in as much as I can and end my time here well. Robert, the mission's Africa director, is visiting from Nairobi and I've asked to meet with him. It's the last Thursday in November, and we're sitting in the living room of the house where he's staying. The low drone of a machine at the workshop hums nearby. Without a fan, it isn't much cooler in here than being outside. Walking over, I could feel the humidity seeping through my dress.

'Thanks for taking the time to meet with me, Robert,' I say, not sure how direct to be. Robert is greying at the temples of his light-brown hair and appears relaxed in short sleeves and slacks.

'Happy to do it. What did you have in mind?'

'Well, though it's been hard at times, I've loved being in Bundibugyo. The beauty is spectacular and the warmth of Ugandans, they've won me over.' I look at him. He nods in agreement. 'After Christmas in London, I'll be heading back to New York. It's been great living in Africa again, but I don't feel drawn to go back to Nigeria. Am wondering if there might be other roles within the mission that I ought to –'

'What was that?' Robert exclaims. He bolts upright and jerks his head towards the screened window.

Hearing a rustling sound, I follow his gaze. A long, dark creature as thick as my bicep is snaking around the stem of a bougainvillea bush, its muscled body gliding past the delicate magenta flowers. We both jump up.

'Let's get a *ponga*,' he bellows.

We dash outside, Robert waving a machete he found under the kitchen sink. As we round the corner with the bush in sight, the coils of a tail disappear into the roof's rafters.

'That was a cobra,' declares Robert. 'Definitely a cobra.' I don't argue. My heart is racing. We stand there looking up, straining to see into the blackness, but the snake is gone, and our being there doesn't make it re-emerge. Giving up after a few minutes, Robert and I go back in and try to resume our meeting. I keep glancing at the exposed beams above us, half-expecting the snake to reappear dangling overhead.

After a distracted half hour, still unsure about what I might do if I were to return to East Africa, I head back to the duplex. Alone, my tummy begins to churn now that the reality of coming that close to a cobra hits me. I'm glad it wasn't slithering up the wall outside my home, but its sighting is a reminder of how close the threat of danger lurks here. I realise how fortunate I am that I've not encountered snakes much before now. A young man working in our yard once discovered several garden snakes hidden among the stones close to our latrine. Fortunately, he told us after he'd killed them. He claimed they were harmless, but left the gory evidence for us to see. Then one morning at breakfast, John, Pat's houseworker, told us about finding one under his bed the night before, as he and his wife lay down to sleep. He used a *ponga* to eliminate that snake, but the whole episode sounded gruesome and terrifying.

Sobered, I begin preparing lunch. With wobbly hands, I wash and cut some cabbage. As I start on the carrots, I hear my screen door opening, and then footsteps. Odd. People rarely enter the duplex without first identifying themselves. I look up to see Scott pulling back the curtain separating the greeting room from the living room. His jaw is tense, his brow furrowed.

He doesn't say anything right away. Not sure how to interpret this unusual visit, I decide not to mention the cobra.

'Scott, what's up?' I ask, trying to sound relaxed.

'Well,' he says, his voice thick and heavy, 'I'm not planning on making house visits to everyone but since your background is in public health, I thought you'd want to know.'

'Know what?' I ask, unsure what this is about.

He clears his throat. 'The CDC have identified the disease killing people in Kikyo.'

'Oh, really? What is it?'

He swallows and then says flatly, 'It's Ebola.'

I don't respond for a few seconds.

'Ebola? Really? It's Ebola in Kikyo? Not typhoid, like Jonah thought?' My hands still unsteady, I set aside the carrots and try to focus on what Scott's saying. Tension extends across my shoulders.

'It's definitely Ebola. Ebola haemorrhagic fever. It's usually highly fatal. This seems to be a less deadly strain. That's why it's taken so long to identify it. UNICEF are flying in tomorrow to assess the situation. We'll know more once they get here.'

'How is Ebola transmitted?' My mind has slowed down and I'm fuzzy on the details, but I should know this. I recall a photo I once saw on the cover of *The New York Times* magazine years before of a healthcare worker wearing a space-like suit to protect against this disease. I wept when I reached the end of that stirring piece of journalism and learned that the physician in charge of that Ebola outbreak had died of the disease. I think it even happened in northern Uganda. I don't mention any of this to Scott.

'It's viral and is spread through contact with body fluids: blood, saliva, sweat, tears, those kinds of things. It's extremely infectious. Those who prepare the dead bodies of people who've died from it can also get it. We're not sure how it gets into humans, probably through contact with bats.'

The tension spreads to the base of my neck.

The news about Ebola is frightening. That said, it's in a village many kilometres from here. I'm still thinking about the live cobra I saw an hour ago. A menacing snake is lurking somewhere in the rafters of a house very near this one. I wonder about blood, though. The Ebola I read about caused blood to ooze out of people.

'Are they sure it's really Ebola, Scott? Did you and Jennifer see people bleeding when you were at Kikyo?'

'We didn't see blood, but some patients reported it in their urine and stool. The clinical officer in charge told us he'd seen blood in some people's vomit. That's never a good sign. Yes, Ebola has been confirmed all right,' he concludes. 'The Ministry of Health plans to announce it later today, at a press conference in Kampala.'

The team meeting that afternoon is subdued. Scott tells everyone about this particular strain of the disease. It seems less fatal than the Ebola that's been seen before. This probably explains why Ebola was ruled out when the CDC ran their initial labs but blood tests from more recent deaths have now verified it.

'We're not sure what having Ebola in Bundibugyo will mean for us as healthcare workers. Jennifer and I went to Kikyo on Monday and cared for some of the patients there. The Ministry of Health will probably ask us to help with the situation. However, if anyone wants to leave the district until this blows over, you should do so. We don't want anyone to stay who doesn't want to.'

'We've decided to end the semester at Christ School tomorrow and send the students home early,' Kevin announces.

His wife, JD, explains, 'We're leaving for Kampala on Monday, after all the grades are in. My mother doesn't want her grandchildren anywhere near Ebola.' She adds, 'Nor do I.'

I wonder if they aren't overreacting. I'm worried, but Kikyo is in a very remote area. It's hard to get to, tucked away high up in the mountains, and many kilometres from the main road in and out of the district. Apart from Jennifer and Scott, none of us have been anywhere near these patients. I'm the only other person on the team who has ever even been to Kikyo and that was months ago.

I turn to Scott. 'Pat and I are planning a party in the HIV clinic tomorrow, for me to say good – '

'Cancel it. I doubt many will come. When this news gets around, people won't leave their homes. Definitely cancel it.' He's so emphatic I don't push back, but look away, my face smarting.

The British UNICEF country director and an American nurse, two blonde-haired, battle-hardened women, fly in the following day and waste no time in assessing the situation. Scott and Will, a physician assistant on our team, take them up to Kikyo. Before evening, these out-of-town visitors make plans to set up an isolation ward there and another at the hospital. They expect an influx of patients. A truckload of supplies from *Médecins Sans Frontières* (MSF), along with their Ebola-experienced staff who have recently contained an outbreak in the Democratic Republic of the Congo, will arrive tomorrow. They advise the district director of health to cancel the programme planned to commemorate World AIDS Day, which also happens to be tomorrow, 1st December. For once it was going to occur on time. Not any more.

We are bracing for a medical crisis.

The next day, Saturday, instead of joining in to celebrate the progress made to tackle AIDS here, I make my way to Nyahuka market. After buying some beans to take to families at the health centre, I pass Jonah's home, which is next door. Mellen is out in front, with her youngest perched on her right hip. I wonder how long she'll be able to carry her like this, as her pregnancy is starting to show. Mellen seems downhearted.

'How are things, Mellen?'

'Not good. Not good at all,' she says in a hushed voice.

'What's wrong?'

'Jeremiah died last night. The funeral is today.'

'Jeremiah died?' I say, gasping. 'Goodness.'

'He was like a father to Jonah,' Mellen continues, 'ever since the time Jonah lost his own father. When he got sick, Jonah cared for him at home, and then when he was in the hospital. Now, he won't even be able to attend the funeral. He went to Kampala to pick up our first daughter from school.' Her voice tapers off. 'This is terrible,' she whispers.

'Oh, Mellen, I'm so sorry.' I shudder.

Muhindo Jeremiah is a prominent person here. I don't know him, but had heard he'd been in the hospital for the last ten days. He's been fighting for his life and people have been talking about him. As is true so often, when a disease affects those with power and status, we take more notice. Besides Jonah and Scott, the medical superintendent also took care of Jeremiah.

News of Jeremiah's death is chilling.

Could Ebola have killed him?

That evening, Moses and his family come for dinner. Moses, who assembles mama kits now that Alex is gone, arrives promptly at 6.30 with his wife and four of their children. All are scrubbed, smelling of soap and wearing their finest clothes. As we did with Jonah's family, we eat Nigerian stew with lots of beef and rice. There's enough left over to send them home with another meal. Though we try to keep things light-hearted, our conversation is strained. No one mentions Ebola.

Around 9.00, Pat and I drop them at home. As we approach Nyahuka, we find the roadside filled with people, strange for this time of the evening, their bodies shadowy and slow-moving in the limited light. It's dark except for our headlights and those of a pick-up truck soliciting final passengers. When we reach the taxi park, I see something I never would have imagined. There, projected onto a large screen, is a film which is describing the seven layers of protection that are essential when one comes into contact with Ebola or suspected Ebola patients: two pairs of gloves, wellington boots, a gown, a cap, goggles and a face mask. Above the din of a generator is a narrator with a middle-

America accent. He sounds like the same one who explained science films I watched in primary school. In this context, his dull, flat voice comes across as a subtle threat. I wonder how people here would be able to afford even one or two of these layers, let alone seven.

It's a surreal moment. Most who are watching probably can't understand more than a few words Mr Science is saying, but the images are powerful and captivating, seductive, even. Throngs of people are held as if spellbound, the voice and pictures mesmerising them. Though I've only lived in Bundibugyo for two years, I sense something is happening here that has no precedent.

The following morning, Scott and Jennifer summon us to gather at their home before church. On a team where most events, including birthday parties and meetings, are scheduled weeks in advance, assembling like this is unusual. Noticing red rings around Jennifer's eyes, I don't have to wait long to find out the cause.

'We have to put our kids on a plane and get them out of here,' she tells us, tears welling up. 'I hate the thought of being separated from them, but it's the wise thing to do. UNICEF and MSF are mandating it.'

I listen, confused.

'All of you have to leave Bundibugyo except me and Jennifer,' Scott explains. 'Will can stay if he wants, too. Since we're all clinicians, the Ministry of Health may need our help.'

'I'm staying,' Will says, without hesitating. I notice that since I'm not a clinician, Scott doesn't give me the option of staying, despite my public health training. I don't protest.

'OK, but the rest of you must leave. It's not safe to be here. We don't know how widespread this is or how long it will last. MSF have even set up an isolation unit in Kampala, at Mulago, just in case. They're taking every precaution. Jonah is too. He's got malaria so he admitted himself. He wants to be careful, like us. Since we treated patients, we may have been exposed, but it's unlikely. We were very careful, but that was before we knew what this was.'

'How long do we have?' I ask, my thoughts focusing on practicalities as a way of trying to remain in control of these fast-moving events.

Jennifer interjects, 'Well, you were planning to leave Uganda later this month anyway, but you shouldn't wait till then. Kim, you too, since your time as a teacher is ending as well. First, we think you should all spend a few days in Jinja, at the resort. That will give everyone some time together. Then, after you both leave, the rest of the team will stay in Kampala, at least for a few weeks, until this all blows over.' She pauses and then adds, 'I'm going to see if MAF can get a plane here on Tuesday.'

'This Tuesday?' I ask, in disbelief. 'How about Wednesday?'

'We think the team should leave together on Tuesday,' she says, her tone signalling this is non-negotiable. 'That will give you a couple of days to pack and say goodbye.'

A couple of days? Is this really happening? My throat tightens and my mind starts to panic, overwhelmed by a flood of sadness and dismay all at once. I'm not ready to leave here in a couple of days. I have plans for finishing well. I want to make good memories with people I care deeply for, people that I'll probably never see again. I was counting on having almost three weeks. That Ebola is in Bundibugyo has changed all of that. This place is far less safe than I realised, but I didn't come here thinking I was putting my life on the line. I didn't come here to die. Or did I? After all, part of why I returned was to learn how to die to my selfish ambitions, but I never once thought that living here might threaten my actual life.

Later at church, during the time for prayer requests, I raise my hand and stand, clutching a tissue. Feeling everyone's eyes on me, I can barely speak. I fight to keep my voice from breaking.

'My time in Bundibugyo is ending. I'm leaving this week.' Starting to choke up, I keep it short. I don't want to cry. 'Thank you for allowing me to be a part of this community. *Weebale mono.*' I drop to my seat and bow my head, hiding my face. The pastor thanks me and as he prays, tears fall onto my lap. I brush them away before he finishes.

After lunch, unable to even think about packing and wanting to deny what's going on, I bike down to Christ School to see some of my friends there. I tell the girls I'm leaving, but don't bring up Ebola. Riding home to make dinner, I run into Kim walking on Nyahuka road. She flags me down.

'Have you heard the latest news?'

'No, what news?' I ask tentatively, my hands gripping the handlebars more tightly, afraid to hear what else may be coming.

'Jennifer couldn't get a plane on Tuesday. We're leaving tomorrow at 4.00.'

'Tomorrow at 4.00?' I repeat in disbelief, my insides quaking. I cycle the rest of the way reluctantly, as if until I get there, I can suspend the fact that I now have less than twenty-four hours remaining. More tears come, these ones blurring my vision, and as I ride, I lift my eyes up to the mountains pleading to God for help.

I stay up until 2.00 emptying shelves and drawers, shoving clothes into suitcases, discarding many others, and consolidating the important content from two years of Kwejuna files into a single box to pass on to Scott. When I finally collapse into bed, my sleep is fitful and uneven. I rise at dawn feeling groggier than if I hadn't tried to sleep at all. My eyes are hot and my eyelids are swollen from all the crying I've done.

I spend the precious remaining hours making the rounds to say farewell. I cycle back to Christ School for some final moments there. I hug the girls one last time. I head to Kisembo's drug shop. His storefront is open but only his assistant is there. She doesn't know where he is or when he'll be back. I leave her with a thank you message for him.

Saying goodbye to Masika is the hardest. I find her in her salon in the market, the smell of pressed hair and chemicals surrounding her. We greet each other as usual, but instead of making small talk, I steer the conversation to Ebola.

'Masika, you know about Ebola, don't you?'

She nods. 'They think it killed Jeremiah, isn't it?'

'Seems so. It's a very serious disease.' I look straight at her, cringing inside due to what I'm about to tell her. 'Because of Ebola, I have to leave sooner than I was expecting. Much sooner.'

'When will you be going?'

I take a slow breath before continuing. 'I'm leaving today. This afternoon.'

'Today?' I watch, uncertain, as she registers this information. Her eyeliner begins to run.

'We have to leave together. We're all going. Except Scott and Jennifer and Will. The plane is coming at 4.00.'

As I'm speaking, she starts sobbing.

'Who will take care of me when you're gone?'

'Masika, you know God is the one who cares for you. That won't change because I'm going.' She grabs me, holding me tightly, her body heaving. I have so much I'd like to say. I want to thank her for the ways she's helped me understand this community, for all the different places we've ventured to on motorcycles, and for the many women we've sat with and tried to support. In the end, between her tears, I can only embrace her.

Four o'clock comes too soon. When we get to the airstrip, I watch Jennifer put her children on the plane. Gone are the red eyes I saw on Sunday. Her oldest is in Virginia with her mother, but these three have never been apart from her or Scott before. I wonder if they realise the seriousness of what's happening. She gives me a tight hug.

I choose a seat in a row all to myself on the left towards the back. Even when we are taxiing, Jennifer, watching the plane from the airstrip, maintains her composure. She reminds me of Mum not crying in public at Papa's funeral. I still don't know how she did it.

As we lift off, I press my face to the small window, looking down at our Ugandan friends below one final time, and weep and weep.

It is silent but violent.

I feel robbed, but also guilty.

Why are we able to fly away from this deadly threat and leave behind the people we love and came to serve? After all, for those who live here, facing this disease must be terrifying for them too. And why am I, the sole African in our group, not insisting that I stay? As the plane climbs higher and higher, I fixate on the airstrip until it disappears as a blur in the distance.

# 26
# The Response

We spend that night in Kampala and head to the resort outside Jinja the following afternoon. I'm grateful to have a few more days left in Uganda but am withdrawn, dazed and not engaging much. We're here to debrief and come to terms with the surreal events of the past few days. Jennifer's wise idea. Being on the edge of Lake Victoria, absorbing the beauty, swimming in the pools and eating fresh fish, all are meant to serve as a distraction from the Ebola outbreak that has struck our district. Yet, as the sun slips below the horizon forming a stunning reflection on the water, I can't help but think of the people I didn't get a chance to see one last time: Jonah, Mellen, Joseph and Kisembo. I promise myself I'll phone them all tomorrow.

After dinner, once the children are in bed, we adults gather to talk about how we're doing. Listening to my teammates voice fear and confusion, I'm overwhelmed with sorrow. My eyelids are heavy, my throat dry like sandpaper, and my head clogged, as if jammed with soaked cotton wool. Anger simmers inside me, like a pot of soup on a fire about to reach a boiling point. The rawness of my emotions feels dangerous. I want to lash out. But at whom? The others around me? God? At the same time, I don't trust myself. How will lambasting the situation make any of this right? For me, or for those facing the horrors of Ebola in Bundibugyo? I say little. Hot tears seep into my eyes, which are raw and sore. I wipe them away. After an hour of being together, with me erupting at one point trying to find someone to blame, we finish with prayer and head to our rooms.

I'm glad to be alone. At the same time, I dread the long night ahead. I fear sleep won't come, despite my emotional and physical exhaustion. I lie down and quiet my mind by trying to be still, but the crickets outside have formed a chorus and are determined to keep singing. Unsettled, I get up to use the toilet. Then, I hear a voice outside my door.

'Pamela, it's Pat. Can I come in?' She's probably having trouble falling asleep too.

'Hold on a second.' I wash my hands. When I unlock the door and open it, Pat pushes past me. She collapses on the bed.

'You OK?' Perplexed, I look at her hunched over.

She lifts her head. 'Jennifer just called.'

'What's up?' I ask, with some hesitation.

'It's terrible.' Her hands cover her face.

'I know. Ebola's terrible.'

'Not just that,' she blurts out, dropping her hands into her lap. 'Jonah's dead.'

'Dead?' I slump down beside her. 'What? Are you sure?'

'Jennifer says he's dead,' Pat insists, her eyes hollow, terrified.

'How can he be dead? I thought he had malaria. Wait, who can we call? Look, let's call Mellen.' I dial Mellen's number, my fingers stubborn and awkward on the keypad. After several tries, the phone rings and I hear a recorded message: 'The number you are calling is not available at the moment. Please try again later.' I listen to it twice before I hang up, bewildered. I shake my head, still in a state of disbelief. Who else can I phone?

'Let me call Kisembo. It's almost 10.00. Do you think it's too late?' Answering my own question, I call him anyway.

'Kisembo, good evening. Sorry to disturb you. This is Pam.Ella.'

'Pam.Ella. How are you?' His voice is thick with sleep. Still, I launch ahead.

'I just received some news about Dr Jonah. Have you heard any news about him?'

'News? What news is that?' he asks, sounding a little more awake.

I don't answer right away, reluctant to share information about Jonah that I'm struggling to accept myself. Restraining my sadness so he won't hear my voice cracking, I announce, 'I heard Jonah is late. Have you heard that?' A long silence follows as I wait for him to respond.

'Let me check. I'll phone you back.'

I turn to Pat, her face tear-stained. 'Kisembo hasn't heard but he'll try to find out.' Sniffling, I wonder aloud, 'Who else can we call?'

'Will?' Pat suggests hesitantly. I call Will. He answers right away.

'Hello? Pamela?' He sounds as if he has a cold.

'Is it true?'

'Yes,' he says, his voice choking with tears. 'MSF at Mulago called Jennifer.'

'But how? How did it happen?'

'We don't know yet. The family doesn't want anyone here to know yet either.'

'We tried calling Mellen but her phone was switched off.'

'This is all so, so unbelievable. Listen, I've got to go.' His voice fades. I drop the phone and grab onto Pat, my mind suspended in a faraway place somewhere between grief and despair.

\* \* \*

From August 2007 to February 2008, Ebola virus disease struck 131 people in Bundibugyo, killing forty-two.[1] Excluding Jonah, this included thirteen other healthcare workers.[2] No one could have foreseen the Ebola outbreak in Bundibugyo. Yes, Ebola was highly contagious and deadly, and well-known to infectious disease specialists, but it had only ever appeared in Uganda once before, in 2000. That was the outbreak I had read about in *The New York Times* magazine[3] when Ebola killed 224 people across three northern districts.[4] Seven years later Bundibugyo was hit. A new strain of Ebola emerging within the same country in a different location in less than a decade had never occurred before, until now.

The early symptoms of Ebola are consistent with malaria, making it difficult to diagnose. Common signs at the start are the sudden onset of fever, chills, headache and weakness. A sore throat, nausea, vomiting and stomach pain follow. Bleeding often comes in the later stages, and in Bundibugyo this was the case among more than half of those who died.[5] Besides touching patients with Ebola, in this outbreak the main way Ebola was transmitted was through washing and dressing the bodies for burial of those who had died from the disease.[6]

Just how Ebola crossed over into humans in Bundibugyo remains unconfirmed, though wildlife probably transmitted it in the Semuliki National Park. The index patient was a twenty-six-year-old woman who died in early August. Five others in her home died shortly after her, leaving three who lived. Despite the presence of spears in that home, these survivors denied that any hunting, illegal in national parks, had taken place.[7]

Once *Bundibugyo ebolavirus* made the leap into humans, the lack of basic sanitation in the clinics was almost certainly a factor in the spread of the disease. The most fundamental infection control procedures such as handwashing between patients and wearing gloves occurred sporadically in Bundibugyo's health centres and at the hospital.

For this reason, though we'll never know for sure, the difference between Jonah surviving and succumbing to Ebola may have come down to a pair of gloves, worth a handful of pennies. After his death, Scott recalled that on a day when he and Jonah had both gone in to care for Jeremiah, between those visits, Jonah had gone in alone. Jonah told him that when he noticed his friend was having difficulty breathing, to provide some relief, he adjusted Jeremiah's face mask – with his bare hands – because he couldn't find any gloves at the hospital in those moments. This may seem careless for a physician, but touching patients without protection was standard practice in Bundibugyo, where the government wasn't able to meet the need for gloves and other basic medicines. The entire Ugandan Ministry of Health is severely underfunded, operating on a budget then that was a quarter of what was needed to provide a minimal basic health programme.[8]

Jeremiah died the day after Ebola was identified as the cause of the mysterious deaths that had been occurring. By then, Jonah, already harbouring the virus, had left the district and was in Kampala. Ironically, because he died in Kampala, his death was not counted in the official death toll.

\* \* \*

The morning after learning of Jonah's death, I retreat into a private sorrow. While others sun themselves by the pool or try to ignore the awful news through forays into novels or competitive games of water polo, I escape to my room. I cry, try to pray and cry some more. Tears fall without restraint until exhaustion overtakes me. When I awake, with swollen eyelids and a headache that feels like a machete is cutting my head in two, I brace myself for the possibility of more deaths of other people I know.

As I'd done when I learned that Nightie's mother had passed away, I search for photos of Jonah on my laptop. I don't have many, but find several of him taken the day the paediatric and maternity building opened. Looking at them over and over again, I try to convince myself that his presence in front of my eyes denies the reality that he's gone. My favourite one was taken after all the speeches were over. When the party was beginning, he and Jennifer, both beaming at the camera with a blend of unrestrained happiness and satisfaction, had posed for a headshot. What was Jonah thinking about in those moments? How he might influence medicine here in the future? How the new building would transform healthcare at Nyahuka? Recalling the tie and sharp doctor's coat he wore that day, and how proud we all were, the joy of that wonderful afternoon seems fleeting now, and very distant.

After lunch, several of us go into Jinja, the nearest town, where we pick up the national daily, the *New Vision* newspaper. The Ebola outbreak is featured in great detail on the front page and inside the centre spread. Devouring the reports, I flinch when I notice some inaccuracies, one of which is a photo of another health worker, also called Jonah, who died of the disease as well. The story has wrongly identified him as Dr Jonah. As I take in the Ebola coverage in print, my anguish about Jonah's death escalates. My sadness is stirred up. This story is far more to me than a gripping or newsworthy account forcing Bundibugyo into the national glare of an uncomfortable spotlight. These events concern a tragedy unfolding in a district that until several days ago had been my home. I know these people. Many of them are my friends or colleagues. My heart aches: for the losses they're experiencing, for the horror unravelling in this tight-knit rural community, for their fears and for the uncertainties ahead.

We stop at a popular internet café, where the smell of coffee brewing permeates the space. I slouch over a desktop computer, oblivious to the crafts and snacks I'm usually eager to buy. Desperate for prayer, I begin typing a note to friends in New York, trying to capture the events of the past forty-eight hours so they can know what to pray for. As my fingers fumble over each key, more tears fall, furiously this time, dampening the keyboard.

I call Will every day for the next five days before I leave Uganda.

'You won't believe this,' he tells me in our first conversation since Jonah died. 'The health centre has emptied out. Most of the patients have left, many against our medical advice, and no one's coming in to replace them.'

'Is it that bad?' I ask.

'It is so strange. I've never seen it like this.'

'What's going on? Do people think they'll catch Ebola at the health centre?'

'Ever since people heard about Jonah, they think it isn't safe here any more. It's not logical, because we know he didn't get Ebola at Nyahuka, but it doesn't matter. People are really scared. It's so empty, it feels like a cemetery.' Then he laughs. 'Of course, it isn't. There may be nobody here, but God's still here.'

'What an amazing attitude you have.'

'It's true. God's here and I'll keep coming, to visit the few patients that are left, but I'm also going to start visiting the staff who live next door, to encourage them. They seem pretty freaked out by all of this. They're keeping away too.'

'It's so sad.'

'Jennifer and Scott and I talked last night and agreed that on Sunday, I should visit some churches too, to educate people about Ebola. I want to teach how you can and can't get it. That might help get rid of some of the fear.'

Though most of us left, Will, Jennifer and Scott have remained in Bundibugyo. Jennifer updates their blog,[9] so from a distance I'm able to follow events happening there. A taskforce, made up of representatives from the CDC, MSF, UNICEF, the World Health Organization and the Ministry of Health, descends in the district, determined to halt the spread of Ebola. A mixed crew of expatriates and Ugandans, some of whom contained the previous outbreak in northern Uganda, meet every evening in Bundibugyo Town to share updates on the status of the epidemic and make administrative decisions about how best to control the situation.

Jennifer documents Jonah's funeral, which takes place on Friday, three days after his death and four days after we were evacuated, with a lengthy post and photos from the sombre affair. Held in the grounds of Bundibugyo Hospital, three other hospital employees who also died from Ebola are buried alongside him in the compound. His corpse came from Kampala in a sealed coffin. Infection control personnel layered in half a dozen types of protective gear lowered his body into the ground.

Most people stayed away.

If Jonah had died from anything other than Ebola, a vast and public outpouring of grief would've marked the passing of Bundibugyo's most celebrated son. Instead, only a handful of bystanders bear witness. One of them is the medical superintendent at Bundibugyo Hospital. When he came down with Ebola, he had shut himself away in his home across the street. Scott visited him every day, leaving food outside his door. To everyone's great relief, he eventually emerged from his self-imposed isolation, weak but disease-free and alive. Jennifer notes that he is one of the courageous few who turn up at the funeral.

Mellen and her five girls, several of whom have shaved heads which can signify mourning, are also among the few who were there, but they weren't able to go anywhere near the casket. As if that isn't painful enough, the community shuns Jonah's family for fear that anyone who comes into contact with them will die too. Following his death, and contrary to what usually happens, Jennifer writes, no one – except she and Scott – comes to offer condolences. Mellen and her children retreat to their family home in the highlands, many kilometres from where they usually live in Nyahuka, next door to the health centre.

Mellen was one of the people I wasn't able to say goodbye to. Following our conversation on my last Saturday when she told me Jeremiah had died of Ebola, which meant Ebola was now much closer than we'd realised, I never saw her again. My small gesture of condolence is to ask Pat to give her the extra roll of material left over from the aprons, to use for her nursery school students' uniforms.

Recalling that vibrant blue colour I chose for those aprons takes me back to that fantastic farewell with the TBAs. Despite their shock at my imminent departure and the sadness which I believe I caused, what has stayed with me are their many hugs and good wishes, the photos of them all dressed in their new garb, the lunch outside afterwards and the unexpected afterparty with the dancing! I remember how they led me around the community centre, singing and swaying, and chuckling at my awkward dance moves. And then, the money they all contributed. Yes, my time in Bundibugyo has ended on a terribly tragic note, but it is the image of these jubilant, faithful, and big-hearted women – their faces lit up with joy, their gift to me of belonging and their role in bringing forth life – that I want to hold on to as my enduring memory of this beautiful place.

# Afterword

A year and a half after that awful flight out of the district, I was able to return for a visit. Bundibugyo had changed, mostly in encouraging ways. The grant supporting the Kwejuna Project, extended one final time, had come to an end. Scott, with Joseph as his trustworthy assistant, had capably overseen the programme and supported the health workers. Days before I arrived, at the close of the fiscal year, the mission transferred full ownership and management of Kwejuna to the Ministry of Health. Rather than experiencing the sense of loss which I'd anticipated, I was at peace. Scott and Jennifer's original intention was for the mission to establish a district-wide HIV prevention programme, make it as sustainable as possible, and then turn over all programmatic aspects and control of the funds to Ugandans. They'd achieved that goal.

This meant five years after Kwejuna began, the prevention of mother-to-child transmission of HIV was now embedded within prenatal care clinics in Bundibugyo.[1] Training had taken place for many health workers, including that which I'd been a part of with the TBAs, and supplies of AIDS drugs[2] and HIV test kits were coming from Kampala somewhat steadily through systems the Ministry of Health had established. Mothers and other family members living with HIV were receiving life-extending medicines at two thriving AIDS clinics. Peer educators, also living with HIV and trained with funds from EGPAF, were teaching in these clinics, offering health education sprinkled with large doses of encouragement.

Another major change occurring in Bundibugyo was that government-issued electricity was making its way over the mountains.[3] Giant steel towers, some already connected with necklaces of wires, dotted the roadside. Power should radically improve the quality of life for people here. However, if the situation in Kampala – where scheduled power outages and back-up generators are ubiquitous – is any indication, I fear the supply won't be reliable. Furthermore, having consistent electricity may become an expense that only the well-to-do can afford.

Sadly, impending electrical power has assaulted the landscape. Gone are many of the roadside banana trees whose leaves once waved so proudly. Much of the elephant grass lining the way is also no longer there. With many trees cleared, the beauty and shade they provided along the road have become casualties too. Even the imposing mango tree in front of the Christ School gate that I rode past on my first morning with Jennifer and many times after that, where I would often meet Masika, is no more. The main road remained rugged and rocky, but there was renewed talk of paving it at last.[4]

As for the legacy of the Ebola outbreak eighteen months removed, I sensed its impact was real but muted. The residents in Bundibugyo had fought back as a community, eliminated the deadly virus and were soldiering on. Direct talk of those events was almost non-existent. However, in my humble observations, people seemed less joyful, more cautious and not as carefree, as if the grief had seeped into their collective psyche.

Despite the hints of melancholy, there were many glimpses of God's grace. Unlike Jonah, some health workers contracted Ebola and survived. The clinical officer in charge at Kikyo, who treated more patients with Ebola than any other health worker during the outbreak, by a miracle did not die. His courage secured for him a scholarship to medical school from monies donated to the Dr Jonah Memorial Leadership Fund, one of several funds which Jennifer and Scott set up in the weeks following Jonah's death. My friend Kisembo was another survivor. It turns out when I called him that evening and told him Jonah had died, he was in the isolation unit at Bundibugyo Hospital, battling for his own life. He has gone on to make a full recovery.

Masika, thankfully, was not directly impacted by Ebola. She was continuing to joyfully serve women in her hair salon. As for Mellen, three and a half months after Jonah's death she gave birth to a son. Named after his father, his arrival was the son this family had long waited for. When I met him, his large inquisitive eyes, wide smile and round face – all features so like that of his father – were a daily reminder that the spirit of Dr Jonah lives on. Mellen had remained in Nyahuka and her nursery school had continued to thrive. Fees for her six children, covered until they each completed secondary school, were coming from the Jonah Kule Family Care Fund.

Except when visiting Mellen and meeting her son, no one talked of Jonah's absence. Yet he was hard to ignore. On the side of the hospital property next to the car park and only partially hidden behind an outpatient building, his grave – along with those of the three other healthcare workers buried there – served as a painful reminder of the human toll Ebola had taken here.

Reflecting on my time in Bundibugyo, there are moments when I'm tempted to become bitter or resigned due to the many wrongs that seem to coalesce in this out-of-the-way place. The needs here are enormous and I discovered that advancing global health in Africa's pearl exacted a great price, and not just for the patients. Yet, to have played a small role in making a difference in the lives of some mothers living with HIV and to have encouraged lay midwives to continue being faithful to their calling was an enormous privilege.

I received far more from this experience than what I offered. Living among the Babwisi and Bakonjo gave me a deep respect for their determination to thrive in the face of immense daily hardships. Despite being materially poor, their consistent joy renewed my belief in the common grace that God gives us all.

Their relationally rich way of life heightened my appreciation for what really matters, and entering into the rhythm of a team of passionate individuals committed to the greater good exposed my need for, and deepened my desire for, authentic community. So, as my time was winding down in Bundibugyo, I'd felt a tug to return to East Africa with the mission; hence my conversation with Robert. I didn't know if this would pan out, but if it did, I thought I might only be back in New York for a year or so before leaving again.

But it was not to be.

After Ebola, I flew to London to spend Christmas with my family. There, I had time and space to grieve before preparing to re-enter New York. I didn't yet have a job or even clarity about what sort of work I might pursue, but I had an apartment to return to and a church to reconnect with.

The day before Christmas Eve, I was walking in a park with my sister. The air was damp and chilly, and my coat wasn't warm enough to keep us outside for long. We were strolling down an incline, soon to turn back towards home, when she asked me, 'What are you going to do for work when you get back to New York?'

'I really don't know, but I'm sure God will provide something. I'm trusting Him.'

I meant what I said. Still, it sounded a bit wistful. I even wondered if I was being too passive. However, an older, wiser soul who was a dear friend had told me months before when I was starting to wonder what might be next after Bundibugyo, 'Don't fret about the next thing. Wait for it. God will bring it.'

And bring it He did, for later that day, I received an email from someone at my church, inviting me to apply for a position that they were looking for a woman to fill. Though unsure if this would be right for me, I began praying and mulling over the possibility. Everyone I spoke to about it, including Jennifer and Scott, encouraged me to apply. So, I submitted my application, went through the interview process, and got an offer. Taking this job was huge because it meant stepping away from my public health career and into a leadership development and pastoral care role. Yet I had a deep conviction it was the right thing to do.

Besides changing my vocation, after the richness of life in Uganda, I knew when I returned to New York there was no going back to the one-dimensional routine I'd had in the Bronx. On the other hand, I couldn't deny the fact that I'd re-entered the pace and pressures of life in the big city, so I needed to be intentional about making different life choices. I began by prioritising self-care. Coming alive in the presence of the beauty of God's creation, something which had been awakened in Bundibugyo, led me to begin walking daily in the park near my home. I reconnected with old friends and invested in new, life-giving relationships. I sought to embrace a weekly sabbath so I could stop, rest, delight in and contemplate God's goodness to me. I took regular times of retreat away from the city for refreshment and renewal. I also discovered a latent interest in writing, which took the forms of journaling, blogging and essay writing, and then evolved into the telling of this story!

During my tenure in the church role, which was both stimulating and challenging, I continued to explore the possibility of returning to Uganda. At one stage, I contemplated joining a new team that had formed in South Sudan. I also had some conversations about another work option with the mission. Yet, I never got peace about the next 'right' East African endeavour for me, so I remained in New York for eight more years, visiting Nigeria or Uganda when I could.

Three and a half years ago, following another nudge from God, I moved to London. My mum, now in her eighties, settled here after Papa's passing. Though in good health and still active, she was beginning to slow down. Wise friends helped me to recognise how precious these remaining years with her would be, and they were right. Living in London has also brought me closer to the rest of my family, here and in Nigeria, which is now a direct six-hour flight away. Though it was difficult to say goodbye to the vibrant community God provided for me in

New York, the decision to live in London was another call to prioritise relationships, this time with family, and trust God with the rest.

And so, the adventure continues, full of what can seem like digressions and deviations and not necessarily the path we'd choose for ourselves. After all, I never expected those first three months in Bundibugyo to be so hard, or that I'd go on to live there for two more years. And then, when I learned of the mysterious disease occurring in the district, it never once crossed my mind that it could be Ebola. But such is the reality of life and health in Africa and, more accurately, such is the nature of a relationship with God. He understands us so well and knows that if He reveals too much of the journey and where the path will lead, many (most?) of us won't be willing to go there. So instead, He gently asks us to walk by faith and, like children, to simply put one foot in front of the other. When we do, however hesitantly we nudge our big toe forward – though the journey may be difficult and perplexing at times – if we hold on, we discover there are always surprising and wonderful gifts along the trail that He wants to give us. The ultimate gift, of course, is that we come to know Him and His love for us more deeply and we learn to move out into the world loving and serving others more and more from the security of that place.

From loss and death, God brought redemption, for the vulnerable out-of-the way community of Bundibugyo, and for me. In spite of poverty, AIDS and Ebola, God transfigured this district's struggles into glimpses of glory and hope. And for me, living alongside those who find themselves on the margins but have an abundant way of life affirmed the high value of people and relationships over the exclusion of chasing ambition and striving for professional success. In serving God, so often we think of it as Him using us to impact others, and no doubt that is a big part of what happens, but it's also just as much or more about how He wants to change us.

# Appendix

I went to Uganda to help to prevent the HIV virus from being transmitted from pregnant mothers to their babies in Bundibugyo. Yet, into this vulnerable community, Ebola had snuck like a scorned lover – uninvited and unannounced. Inflicting its unique danger, it took out the people most intimately involved with those the disease touched: health workers and family members who risked their lives caring for sick relatives.

Could Ebola occur in Bundibugyo again? It's certainly possible, but probably unlikely. Since the outbreak that led to my evacuation, there have been three other small Ebola outbreaks in Uganda, resulting in eighteen cases combined. All have been in areas of the country where the disease had never been seen before. None were caused by the *Bundibugyo ebolavirus* strain.[1] However, Ebola continues to wreak havoc elsewhere on the continent.

The 2007-08 Ebola outbreak in Bundibugyo didn't warrant international attention except among the public health community, but a little more than five years later, the deadliest Ebola outbreak to date began in West Africa. It raged on for more than a year, and by the end of 2014 it had caused a staggering 11,300 deaths, killing 40 per cent of those who got the disease.[2] This unprecedented devastation, occurring in Guinea, Liberia and Sierra Leone and with a scare in Nigeria, highlighted yet again the terrible toll Ebola takes on caregivers. As had been the case before, vulnerable health systems played a culpable role, along with a scarcity of health workers.[3] Following this outbreak, experts warned that other Ebola outbreaks would continue to occur[4] – the question was not if, but when and where.

They were not wrong.

Though not on the scale of that seen in West Africa (fortunately), as I write this, the world's second deadliest Ebola outbreak is occurring in the eastern part of the Democratic Republic of the Congo (DRC). It too has been ongoing for more than a year. As of November 2019, there have been more than 3,200 people infected and more than 2,100 deaths confirmed.[5] So far, it seems to be contained in the DRC, but three cases of Ebola were picked up in the Kasese district of Uganda from a family who had crossed over the border. None of those people survived, and the response identifying contacts was rapid and effective.[6] However, the challenges remain because Uganda shares a 900-kilometre border with the DRC and travel across it, as was true for Nightie's family, is 'often porous'.[7]

Ebola outbreaks, whether relatively small such as the one in Bundibugyo, or on a grander scale like this one in the DRC, are devastating no matter their size. However, an Ebola vaccine is likely to be available soon. The World Health Organization has recently announced that for the first time it has 'prequalified' a vaccine for Ebola, which means it is speeding up the licensing process and enabling UN agencies and the Vaccine Alliance to obtain it for use in countries at risk of outbreaks.[8] Once licensed, a vaccine should dramatically help to curb the spread of Ebola, ultimately saving many lives.

# Glossary

ALS: amyotrophic lateral sclerosis; also called motor neuron disease

ARVs: antiretroviral drugs

BAWILHA: Bundibugyo Association of Women Living with HIV/AIDS

*boda boda*: motorcycle

Bundibugyo: district in western Uganda bordering the Democratic Republic of the Congo

CAO: chief administrative officer, the top official in the district

CDC: Centers for Disease Control and Prevention in Atlanta, GA, USA

duplex: two adjacent homes that share an interior wall in common

EGPAF: Elizabeth Glaser Pediatric AIDS Foundation

*kitabo*: exercise book, often used as a patient's medical chart

*kitenge*: cloth or wrap, usually worn by women or wrapped around babies

Lubwisi: main language spoken in Bundibugyo

*matoke*: mashed green banana; the national dish of Uganda

MAF: Mission Aviation Fellowship, organisation that flies people and items to very remote areas

MSF: *Médecins Sans Frontières*, also called Doctors Without Borders

*muzungu*: white person; foreigner

*ponga*: machete

TBA: traditional birth attendant, also known as a lay midwife

UNICEF: United Nations Children's Fund, formerly called United Nations International Children's Emergency Fund

USh: Ugandan shillings

World Harvest Mission: mission agency based outside Philadelphia, in Jenkintown, PA, USA; now called Serge

# Reflection Questions

Here are questions organised around the book's central themes, designed to invite you to go beyond this story and into your own. You can work through these yourself or talk through them with others who have also read *African Pearl*.

## Community

One of the key attractions of this journey for Pamela was that she would be living and working alongside others in a community. These questions invite you to reflect on her community, your communities, and how you might deepen community in your own context.

### Exploring Community

1. When you hear the word 'community', what do you think of? Take time to acknowledge the different communities you're a part of.
2. Who comprises the community Pamela enters at the start of the book? In what ways is she similar or dissimilar to its members? In what ways is this community life-giving to her?
3. How does Pamela's community change as the narrative progresses? What do we learn about the changing nature of community from her experiences?

### Challenged by Community

4. In what ways is Pamela stretched by living in community? Which of these are good ways? Which of these are difficult for her?

5. What does she learn about herself from living in community? What insights do we gain about the messiness of living in community from this story?

6. What do Pamela's experiences of community (positive and negative) teach us about its importance? What might this suggest for our own well-being and spiritual growth?

### Deepening Community

7. What are some of the tangible ways you have been enriched by the communities you're a part of? In what ways do you resist the challenges of community?

8. Think of two things about yourself that one of the communities you're a part of doesn't know about you. How can you bring more of who you are into these relationships?

9. Probably all of us need to be challenged to engage with others very different from ourselves. Who is someone you could befriend who would stretch you relationally?

## Death, Resurrection and Redemption

Death is a central theme of this narrative. These next questions invite you to linger over the issue of death – something most of us don't like to look long and hard at – in the hope that the process will give way to new insights, signs of resurrection, and hints of redemption.

## Noticing Death

1. Recount a time in your life when you experienced the death of someone you knew personally. What brought comfort from that loss?

2. Think about a time in your life when you had to die to something you held dear. What did that feel like? How did it change you?

3. Think about something (or someone) you may need to die to in your life right now. How might you be more able to let go if you view this process as an invitation to opening yourself up to something new?

## Discovering Resurrection

4. Death makes resurrection possible, but it is still a dark and disorientating time. Who (or what resources) might you seek out to accompany you while you're in this valley where you're having to let go of something (or someone) dear?

5. How might the hope of resurrection encourage you to be patient as you bear the sorrow and pain of loss, given the knowledge that new life is only possible following some sort of death? As you wait for the new thing to emerge, how might you wait 'well'?

6. How might clinging to the reality of life after death make you more willing to die to yourself, in small and big ways, on a regular basis?

## Glimpsing Redemption

7. When we're able to recognise the resurrections that come from dying to our selfish desires, we begin to experience redemption – seeing something good has emerged from something that seemed pretty awful. Where do you see that happening in this story?

8. What are the redemptive experiences that you can point to in your own life? How might these be sources of hope going forward?

# Acknowledgements

The story told here would not have been possible without the generosity of many who supported me financially and prayerfully, enabling me to go to Bundibugyo in the first place. To all of you, I say a big: 'Thank you!' And my journey would've been far different without the warmth and embrace of the teams who welcomed me into their lives once I got there. Much of what we shared together didn't make it into this account, but you all know who you are. I'm humbled to call you my brothers and sisters. I'm also grateful to my Ugandan friends in Bundibugyo who folded me into their rich community.

Much gratitude goes to Dr Bob Fullilove for encouraging me to write a book many years ago. This isn't what we had in mind, but the seed was definitely planted then. This particular book had its origins in the writing workshops at Uptown Writers in Washington Heights. Special thanks to Kathy Crisci and Lori Soderlind for their encouragement and wisdom, as well as Andrea Crawford and Danielle Otieri. I'm also very appreciative for the Redeemer Writers Group, and especially Maria Fee for publishing the first excerpt, which meant so much. Fiction writers in the workshops that form part of the Complete Creative Writing Course in London were key companions in the latter stages of this project.

Thanks to all of you who read the finished manuscript and offered invaluable feedback: Esther Bennet, Linda Dolan, Maggie Hamand, Jo Kadlecek, Jennifer Myhre and Lori Soderlind. Other writers I admire as well – Nana Ekua Brew-

Hammond, Maxine Brown, Michelle Burford and Diane O'Connell – read chapters or the proposal, and offered helpful insights and guidance. Jen Chan supported me from across the miles in Tanzania when we shared our work together. Andi Brindley offered her beautiful home on the Jersey Shore as an ideal place to write, and my times there were a special gift. I'm so very thankful too for other dear friends who were companions on this journey. You regularly asked me about how this project was going, cheered me on from the sidelines, and prayed with and for me: Ann Denise, Chris, Christine, Esther, Faith, Frances, Jo, Linda, Michelle, Pat, Ruth, Ruth Ann and Sonja. I couldn't have got to this point without each of you. Thanks also to Nicki Copeland and her talented team at Instant Apostle for believing in this story and committing to getting it out.

A big thank you goes to my family for their unwavering love and support. Above all, I'm so grateful to God for the journey He has me on and for the desire and opportunities He's given me to share this story. He alone is worthy.

# Endnotes

**Epigraph**

[1] Ruth Haley Barton, 'Are You Longing for More in Church?' 28th May 2019, www.transformingcenter.org (accessed 9th December 2019). Adapted and used with permission.

**6: The News**

[1] J Brooks Jackson et al, 'Intrapartum and neonatal single-dose nevirapine compared with zidovudine for prevention of mother-to-child transmission of HIV-1 in Kampala, Uganda: 18-month follow-up of the HIVNET 012 randomised trial', *The Lancet*, volume 362, 13th September 2003, pp 859-868.

[2] Ibid.

[3] Edward C Green and Wilfred Mlay, 'Let Africans Decide How to Fight AIDS', *Washington Post*, 29th November 2003, pp A23.

[4] Elaine M Murphy, Margaret E Greene, Alexandra Mihailovic and Peter Olupot-Olupot, 'Was the "ABC" Approach (Abstinence, Being Faithful, Using Condoms) Responsible for Uganda's Decline in HIV?' *PLOS Medicine*, volume 9, issue 3, September 2006, pp 1443-1447.

**12: The Illness**

[1] John Wade Long, Jr, *SONSHIP for Africa* (Jenkintown, PA: World Harvest Mission, 1996-2002), pp S16-5. Used with permission.

[2] Ibid, pp S16-3. Scripture quote is NIV 1984.

[3] Ibid. Scripture quote is NIV 1984.

[4] Ibid. Scripture quote is NIV 1984.

### 17: The Visitors

[1] http://www.pedaids.org/pages/mission-statement (accessed 19th January 2015).

### 20: The Doctor

[1] Mukonjo is the singular term for a person from the Bakonjo ethnic group.

### 22: The Celebration

[1] Matthew 13:46.

### 23: The Mystery

[1] Words are from a songbook, *Ebizina By'Obwomeezi Buhyaka MuYesu*, put together as 'a gift to our Ugandan Brothers and Sisters from the World Harvest Mission Team and Prayer Team of 1999'. Copyright details unavailable.

### 24: The Disease

[1] Esther 4:14.

### 26: The Response

[1] Adam MacNeil et al, 'Filovirus Outbreak Detection and Surveillance: Lessons from Bundibugyo', *The Journal of Infectious Diseases*, volume 204, number S761-S767, 2011, p S762.

[2] Joseph F Wamala et al, 'Ebola Hemorrhagic Fever Associated with Novel Virus Strain, Uganda, 2007-2008', *Emerging Infectious Diseases*, volume 16, number 7, July 2010, pp 1087-1092.

[3] Blaine Harden, 'Dr. Matthew's Passion', *The New York Times Magazine*, 18th February 2001, pp 26-31,52,58,62-63.

[4] http://www.cdc.gov/vhf/ebola/outbreaks/history/chronology.html (accessed 18th January 2015).

[5] Joseph F Wamala et al, 'Ebola Hemorrhagic Fever Associated with Novel Virus Strain, Uganda, 2007-2008'.

[6] Ibid, pp 1090-1091.

[7] Ibid, pp1089, pp 1092.

[8] Action for Global Health, Country Briefing, 'Health Spending in Uganda, April 2010', https://actionforglobalhealth.org.uk/ (accessed 19th January 2015), pp 6.

[9] www.paradoxuganda.blogspot.com (accessed 3rd December 2019).

## Afterword

[1] More than 30,000 pregnant women had been tested for HIV, 800 (2.7 per cent) were found to be positive, and 550 took nevirapine when delivering their babies. Almost half of their newborns (246) received nevirapine as well, giving them a real chance to avoid HIV. Source: Scott D Myhre, 'Bundibugyo District PMTCT Summary: 2004-2007', 10th June 2008. Unpublished data; used with permission.

[2] Before I left in 2007, EGPAF had begun to introduce the replacement of single-dose nevirapine (which can contribute to drug resistance) with a combination of antiretroviral drugs taken for longer among pregnant women.

[3] Bundibugyo Electrical Cooperative Society (BECS) runs the distribution of electricity to Bundibugyo and has done so since 2009. As of 2016, it served about 1,500 customers. Geofrey Okoboi and Joseph Mawejje, 'Electricity Peak Demand in Uganda: Insights and Foresight', *Sustainability and Society,* volume 6, number 29, 2016, p 5.

[4] When I visited Bundibugyo in July 2014, the road from Fort Portal to Bundibugyo had been paved.

## Appendix

[1] Centers for Disease Control and Prevention, 'Known Cases and Outbreaks of Ebola Virus Disease', http://www.cdc.gov/vhf/ebola/outbreaks/history/chronology.html (accessed 18th January 2015). There was a *Bundibugyo ebolavirus* outbreak in 2012 in the Democratic Republic of the Congo, resulting in thirty-six cases and thirteen deaths.

[2] Ebola Data and Statistics, World Health Organization, http://apps.who.int/gho/data/view.ebola-sitrep.ebola-summary-latest?lang=en (accessed 27th July 2018).

[3] Peter Piot, Jean-Jacques Muyembe, W John Edmunds. 'Ebola in West Africa: From Disease Outbreak to Humanitarian Crisis', *The Lancet,* volume 14, November 2014, p 1034.

[4] Ibid, p 1035.

[5] https://www.who.int/emergencies/diseases/ebola/drc-2019 (accessed 24th November 2019). The outbreak was declared on 1st August 2018.

[6] https://www.afro.who.int/news/who-regional-director-commends-ugandas-ebola-preparedness-response-0 (accessed 11th September 2019).

[7] Ibid.

[8] 'WHO prequalifies Ebola vaccine, paving the way for its use in high-risk countries', press release, 12th November 2019, https://www.who.int/news-room/detail/12-11-2019-who-prequalifies-ebola-vaccine-paving-the-way-for-its-use-in-high-risk-countries (accessed 14th November 2019).